W9-BSQ-675

Nia Nia, Sarah Lee (Sarah Lee), age 17, Hawaii, USA
Canon EOS Digital Rebel XT (350D), 18–55mm lens,
ISO 800, 1/800 sec. at f/18, no flash
PHOTO © SARAH LEE

Click*

The Ultimate Photography Guide for Generation Now

Charlie Styr with Maria Wakem

AMPHOTO BOOKS
AN IMPRINT OF WATSON-GUPTILL PUBLICATIONS
NEW YORK

Senior Acquisitions Editor: Julie Mazur

Editor: Cathy Hennessy

Art Director: Jess Morphew

Designer: Working Overtime Production

Production Manager: Alyn Evans

First published in the United States in 2009 by Amphoto Books,
an imprint of Watson-Guptill Publications,
the Crown Publishing Group,
a division of Random House, Inc.,
1745 Broadway, New York, NY 10019

www.crownpublishing.com
www.watsonguptill.com
www.amphotobooks.com

Library of Congress Cataloging-in-Publication Data available upon request.
ISBN: 978-0-8230-9237-6

Printed in China

First printing, 2009

1 2 3 4 5 6 7 8 / 15 14 13 12 11 10 09 08

On the cover:
Speed Wobbles, Sean Dalin (sean dalin), age 19, British Columbia, Canada
Canon EOS 20D, 10–22mm lens, ISO 400, 1/6 sec. at f/5, Canon Speedlite 430EX flash
PHOTO © SEAN DALIN

Acknowledgments

My first thanks go to Julie Mazur for seeking me out through Flickr to write this book. Also thanks are due to the great team at Watson-Guptill Publications for seeing the book through to its completion.

Next, I would like to thank Maria Wakem for being a helpful hand during the writing of the book, being a great guide with clear expertise, and for accompanying me into territory I had yet to discover. It was really great to work with you!

I would also like to thank the members of the Teenage Photographers group on Flickr for their support of the book idea, and for those who allowed their photos to be used in this book so that we could show the world the quality of teenage photographers' work.

Last, and most important, I'd like to thank my family and close friends for their support during the creation of the book as a concept, and then during the writing. In particular to my mother, for without her nagging during the summer, the book may never have been completed.

—*Charlie Styr, December 2007*

First and foremost, I would like to thank my husband, Matthew, whose passion and dedication to the photographic profession never ceases to inspire and amaze me. It was through him that I have been blessed to meet such a talented crew of friends and advisors, who have all helped in contributing to this book.

Of those friends, my deepest gratitude goes out to Hyla Dennis, who culled through more than 10,000 images and fielded questions from both parents and teens all over the world to bring the images you see on the following pages to publication.

I would also like to thank Julie Mazur, the team at Watson-Guptill Publications, and my colleagues at *Photo District News (PDN)* for making this book possible. There is not enough room to name each and every one of you, but you know who you are.

Thank you, too, to the many professional photographers who offered their tips and techniques for this book. Your generosity in sharing your knowledge has been invaluable to me.

A final thanks goes to my parents for their support and guidance all these years, and to my favorite teen, my brother Luigi, whose interest in girls and video games most likely outweighs his interest in photography, but I love him just the same.

—*Maria Wakem, December 2007*

Dice Water Splash, Joshua Rozad
(jbr_jbr), age 15, Ontario, Canada
Canon PowerShot S3IS, tripod, ISO 80,
1/250 sec. at f/2.7, on-camera flash
PHOTO © JOSHUA ROZAD

Contents

Click *

Floating Forward, Kirsty Marr (seventy-five),
age 17, Texas, USA
Olympus C-7070 Wide Zoom, ISO 80, 1/15 sec.
at f/2.8, no flash
PHOTO © KIRSTY MARR

Sunset, Charlie Styr (CharlieStyr), age 17, England, UK
A sunset in Mallorca. The photographer climbed a roof to capture this shot.
Fujifilm FinePix S7000, ISO 200, 1/125 sec. at f/2.8, no flash
PHOTO © CHARLIE STYR

Introduction

My interest in photography began when I was around twelve or thirteen, as I started paying more attention to photos in newspapers, old family albums, and the art department at school. It wasn't long before I started taking my own pictures, with a disposable camera, while on vacation. Now, five years and thousands of pictures later, photography has become many things to me—a way to express myself, a way to enhance my creative skills, a way to document precious moments. And you know what? I'm not alone.

In February 2006, I started the "Teenage Photographers" group on Flickr.com (www.flickr.com/groups/teenphotographers), an online photo-sharing community. I invited a few friends to join, and a few months later, we had a hundred or so members. A few months after that, we broke a thousand. Now there are approximately one thousand members and more than 12,000 photos! Turns out, there are a lot of teens out there taking amazing photographs. The group's members are from North America, Europe, South America, Asia, Australia, New Zealand, and Africa—posting photos from every corner of the globe.

As I write this book, Flickr is in the midst of joining forces with Getty Images, the largest, most successful stock agency in the world, to create a special collection of Flickr images, giving teens (and other Flickr members) the potential to make money from their photographs.

These developments show how popular photography has become, and teens like us are taking photographs today like never before. When you think about it, it makes sense. For starters, there are cameras everywhere. Whether you're using high-quality digital single-lens reflex (DSLR) cameras, camera phones, or compact point-and-shoots, there is no limit to where and when you can take great photographs. Since it's all digital, you can take as many photos as you want without worrying about expense, and get instant gratification.

And that's only the beginning: Most home computers come with software to edit your photos, and there are more advanced software programs, too—the creative possibilities are endless. Once you're happy with your shots, you can upload them to Flickr, MySpace, Facebook, deviantART—any of a number of online sites—and become instantly connected to thousands, even millions, of teen photographers all over the world. You can discuss your images, have them critiqued, or have them publicized—everything is possible without ever leaving your room!

Of course, aside from the technology, photography is an art form, and the basics that go into making it an art are still there to be learned. Whether thinking about how to compose a shot, choosing your lighting, picking your subjects, or really seeing the world around you as you set up your frame, you are

joining the long list of photographic legends—from Richard Avedon to Irving Penn—who have helped photography become the creative, dynamic, and powerful art form it is today.

Click is for aspiring and interested photographers, whether you're a beginner picking up a camera for the first time or have been shooting since you were ten. It's both a how-to book and a photo portfolio, packed with amazing examples of what we teens are creating today.

Click starts by breaking down the basics of photography: from picking your first camera to understanding things like shutter speed, film speed, and aperture. It then looks at twenty-six popular photography topics—from creating self-portraits to capturing action to taking extreme close-ups. Each "essay" is packed with techniques, tips, and information you can put to use right away. I gathered information from all sorts of places: my own thoughts and experience, and things I learned from friends on Flickr. After taking photos for a few years, at different events, on vacation, and during everyday life, I have learned some things that I think are worth sharing. If you want more technical details on something discussed in this book, just look online—you'll find many websites and blogs with more extensive articles and guides.

The photographs included are all from the Flickr Teenage Photographers group, taken by teens from all over the world. They are not meant to be "the best" and were not picked out by a panel of professionals, but we think they represent the great range, energy, creativity, and skill to be found in teen photography. For each image, we've included the photographer's name, Flickr screen name (in parentheses), age, where they are from, as well as the photo gear and camera settings used to take the photo—though we can't promise that their Flickr names won't change before this book goes to press!

If you already have a camera, the best thing you can do is get out there and start taking photos. Let this book inspire you, help you, give you ideas, but don't let it take the place of trying things on your own! The more photos you take, the more you'll learn, and the closer you'll come to developing your own style. And don't let this book be your only inspiration—check out photographers' work on the Internet and in books, go see exhibits in your local museum or gallery, and just plain open your mind to the amazing range of styles out there. Pretty soon, you can be part of the world of photography, too, creating your own way of thinking and capturing images. Photography is so much more than just a method of recording moments in time. It is a hobby, an art, even a conversation piece! What have you got to lose? A little time that you would have otherwise spent doing... what? Exactly. We can't wait to see the images you make.

Getting Started
The Basics You Need to Know

1

Interested in photography, but have no idea where to begin? You've come to the right place. Like most things, photography is something you get better at the more you practice. But there are still some basics that any newbie ought to learn. This section lays out all you need to know, from how to choose the right camera to the more technical side of capturing a picture, along with guidelines on everything from exposure to composition. So what are you waiting for?

Farid, Benjamin Ang Zhen Ming (nccair), age 18, Singapore, Singapore
Canon PowerShot S5IS, ISO 200, 1/125 sec. at f/3.5, no flash
PHOTO © BENJAMIN ANG ZHEN MING

Equipment 101

When it comes to photography, equipment matters. You don't have to spend a fortune to equip yourself for a start in imagemaking, but you should make sure you're getting the best equipment possible within your budget. Plan on purchasing key pieces first, such as the camera, then move on to the most useful accessories. Here are some tips to help you get started.

Choosing a Camera

The first thing to start with in photography is deciding which camera to use. Of course, this decision may have been made for you if you were given a camera or are borrowing one from a friend or relative. But if you're looking to buy one, the type of camera you choose is a major decision, and one that will affect your photography for years to come.

Most likely, this decision will be based on the great photographic debate: film or digital? Film and digital cameras work in very similar ways. Both cameras record images mainly using the lens. Light bounces off your subject and through the lens. In a film camera, the shutter opens for a variable amount of time, and the light "burns" the image onto the film inside the camera. This film is then chemically processed to create the final image. A digital camera works in almost the same way, except that instead of a piece of film, there is a digital sensor that senses the light hitting it and then stores this data as an image file readable by your computer.

Each format has its own advantages. Film is generally known for its superior quality, specifically, its ability to capture detail far better than its digital counterpart. With film, the captured image is recorded onto a negative, which can later be processed and printed at various sizes without appearing blurry.

Digital images, however, are composed of pixels—small color samples, or dots, that when put together make up your captured image. The word megapixel (one million pixels) is often used to describe the units that go into the resolution of a camera, or its ability to capture fine detail. The higher the megapixel number of a camera, the more detail it can capture, and the larger you can blow up your image without it appearing blurry.

When the first digital cameras were created about twenty years ago, they were 1 to 2 megapixel cameras, which basically means they were capable of producing 5 × 7 inch high-resolution prints of your images with all details intact. But if you printed your images larger than 5 × 7 inches, they would begin to appear blurry.

Today, technology has advanced at such a swift pace that there are 8 to 10 megapixel digital cameras available at reasonable prices. These cameras should enable you to shoot remarkably sharp images, even when blown up as large as 3900 by 2600 pixels, which is typically good enough for a high-resolution 8½ × 13 print. If you're just starting out in photography, a digital camera is probably the more cost-efficient choice. A film camera allows you to shoot approximately thirty-six photos per roll and requires you to buy, develop, and print each roll, while a digital camera, on average, allows you to shoot about three hundred images on a 1-gigabyte memory card. If you need more space, you can just delete the photos you don't like, download them to your computer, and delete them from your camera. Or you can buy additional or larger memory cards to fit more images. Perhaps the biggest advantage to digital cameras is the instant gratification: you can immediately see your photos to check composition and exposure. Most important, you can print only the photographs you like. This will save you time and money. It is also easier on the environment, as there is less paper waste, and no need for processing chemicals.

When purchasing a digital camera, here are the main things to consider:

1. **How many megapixels do I need?** The first question to ask yourself is, What do you want to do with your pictures once you have taken them? If all you will be doing with your photos is sharing them online with friends and maybe making small prints —5 × 7 inches or less— then a 2- to 5-megapixel digital camera should meet your needs. However, if you want the option of printing out high-quality photos at sizes larger than 5 × 7 inches, then you may want to consider investing in a camera with a higher resolution of, say, 8 to 10 megapixels.

2. **How much can I afford to spend?** The cost of a camera increases along with its megapixel size and number of built-in special features—like *face detection*, which automatically pinpoints and focuses on the faces of your subjects and is great for portraiture, or *image stabilization*, which eliminates camera shake and is helpful when you need to keep the camera steady but don't have a tripod. So choose your price range first, then look at the best options within that range.

3. **What is the zoom range?** How wide and how close up can you get on a shot when using the built-in lens? There are two common types of zoom that you will find on digital cameras, but only one that you should actually use. An optical zoom is preferable because it uses *the actual lens* on the front of the camera to bring the subject closer or farther away, thus keeping the image quality high. Digital zoom does not use the lens. Instead, it *simulates* optical zoom—it pinpoints the center of the picture, crops the surrounding area, and enlarges the subject to fill the resolution and appear closer in the frame. While this process is quick and simple, you lose picture quality because of the simulation, so when given the choice, it's smarter to opt for optical!

4. **What size camera do I want?** Is portability important to you? Do you want a small point-and-shoot camera that you can slip into your pocket and easily be carried with you everywhere you go? Or do you prefer a higher quality, but larger, single-lens reflex (SLR) camera that you will need to carry attached to a strap around your neck or in a small camera bag?

Rainbow Drops, Frida Gruffman (~josse*~), age 19, Skelleften, Sweden
Use the built-in macro mode on a point-and-shoot camera to magnify details in your subject, like these water drops on a CD.
Canon PowerShot S2IS, 1/60 sec. at f/2.7, no flash
PHOTO © FRIDA GRUFFMAN

Finding a Lens

The lens is that concave glass structure on the front of your camera. It refracts light, then channels that light through to the digital sensor (or film) in your camera, thus turning that light into an image. The quality of your lens determines the quality of every photograph you take, so it is an important piece of equipment to consider.

On an SLR camera, the kind of camera used by professionals and serious amateurs, the lenses are interchangeable. This allows you to purchase special-purpose lenses, such as a telephoto lens for zooming in close enough to capture a bird in the distance, or a wide-angle lens to shoot wide enough to show not only the bird but the entire forest.

Most other cameras, including compact point-and-shoots, have fixed lenses. Because a fixed lens is built into the camera, it's not interchangeable (which is why the zoom range question I mentioned earlier is so important). However, you can purchase add-on lenses for more advanced fixed-lens cameras. Add-on lenses are attached to the fixed lens portion of your camera to increase its optical zoom capacity. For example, a high-zoom telephoto lens will allow you to capture a subject from a distance and is useful when photographing birds or other wildlife. A wide-angle zoom lens is great for landscape photography because it increases the width of your frame, allowing you to capture more of the scenery. And a powerful macro zoom lens will enable you to take extremely close-up pictures of anything from flowers to a grain of sand. Unlike a regular close-up shot, a photograph taken with this lens lets you capture the microscopic details that are outside the range of your eyes.

You will need to check with your camera manufacturer or local photography store as to the best add-on lenses for the type of camera you are using and the types of pictures you want to take.

Flash

If you've ever used a camera (and I'm sure you have or you wouldn't be reading this!), you know that a flash is used to provide additional light for a photograph, especially in low-light situations. In almost all compact cameras, the flash will give you good results only if your subject is at least 16 feet (5 meters) away. Many people do not know this, and photos can be ruined by the misuse of flash.

Mod Star, Kaitlyn Bida (K-Annie B), age 17, Ontario, Canada
The subject in this self-portrait was illuminated using her point-and-shoot camera's built-in flash.
Canon PowerShot S3IS, 1/60 sec.at f/2.7
PHOTO © KAITLYN BIDA

Carina, Kristian Sanbaek Solli (kristiansolli), age 17, Blaker, Norway
A 1600-watt professional light, which functions as a huge flash on a stand, was used to light the subject in this portrait, which was shot for a class in portrait lighting.
Nikon D80, 70–200mm lens, ISO 100, 1/160 sec. at f/22
PHOTO © KRISTIAN S. SOLLI

The flash on some cameras may overexpose photographs, making them too bright. This will cause your image to look like a big, white blob, which often happens when your subject is too close. Conversely, if your subject is too far away, the flash will not affect it, and the image will turn out black. If you are shooting in these types of situations, try disabling the flash to use existing light; just look for a button on your camera with a lightning bolt icon or the word *flash*, and press it to turn the flash off.

Of course, there are many situations in which a flash can be useful. If you are trying to photograph your friends dancing at a party, chances are their faces will be difficult to recognize if you don't use it. When you're photographing a subject in harsh, direct sunlight, a flash can be used to fill in the shadows on the face for a more visually appealing portrait. (See page 36 for more on the use of flash.)

Exposure Modes

Familiarizing yourself with your digital camera's exposure modes will help you to determine whether or not you even need a flash for your specific shot. The exact name for each mode may differ depending on the camera manufacturer, but universally, each mode controls the aperture and shutter speed settings to provide optimal results in various lighting situations.

Some of the more commonly used terms for these modes are as follows:

Automatic mode, which, as the name suggests, sets the shutter speed and aperture for you. This mode allows you to shoot without worrying about settings, and lets you concentrate on the composition of an image. If the image you are attempting to capture needs a flash, the flash will automatically fire when you press the shutter (unless you turn it off).

Aperture Priority mode lets you select the aperture needed to obtain the depth of field you want, but the camera automatically sets the best shutter speed to give you a good exposure. As a general rule, use this mode whenever depth of field is most important, such as in a landscape shot.

Scene mode is an umbrella term for a camera's preselected settings, such as landscape, portrait, or night portrait. The number of available scene modes varies from camera to camera. On some cameras, you even have a menu of numerous settings to choose from. However, it is usually obvious by the name of the setting in what situation you should use it.

Shutter Priority mode allows you to choose the shutter speed you need to freeze or deliberately blur subject movement, but the camera automatically sets the most

appropriate aperture for you in order to ensure a good exposure. This mode is most helpful when photographing action scenes, like those discussed in chapter 4.

Manual mode lets you select both the shutter speed and the aperture yourself. Using this mode will require you to have a full understanding of the relationship of aperture to shutter speed, and how together they will affect your final image. If you're just starting out, you may want to use all of the above first, and use this mode only when the others don't give you the results you want.

Most high-end cameras also have custom settings, which basically means you can store your own personal settings for future use. This is helpful when you find yourself using the same settings over and over again.

Tripod and Other Accessories

A **tripod** is an amazing addition to your photography kit. It is a three-legged stand that ensures your camera will stay completely still, without rocking, when you take a picture. If you don't have a steady hand, a tripod is a must-have. It is also essential for low-light conditions, when your shutter speeds will be slower, which means your pictures will be blurry unless your camera is very still. There are lots of tripod styles available, including small portable ones you can throw in a backpack, or even a purse.

With most tripods, you get what you pay for, and some even require you to purchase additional accessories, like a tripod head that attaches the camera to the tripod to keep it steady. If a good tripod is out of your budget range, then simply get creative. Use a tabletop, a step of a ladder, or a fence—any even, flat surface will suffice. (We talk more about how to use your surroundings to your advantage in the self-portrait section on page 56.)

In addition to the tripod and flash, other must-haves include: a camera bag to stow your camera and gear, spare batteries in case yours run out, additional memory cards, and a soft cloth to clean dust off your lens or LCD screen (LCD stands for liquid crystal display, the digital window on your camera that lets you preview and review your images).

STARTER KIT CHECKLIST

- ✳ Camera
- ✳ Tripod
- ✳ Batteries
- ✳ Memory cards or film
- ✳ Lens cloth
- ✳ Camera bag

Basic Tech Terms

The technical concepts in this section may seem confusing at first, but after reading about them a few times and then putting them into practice as you take your own pictures, things will soon click—literally. So don't be intimidated by the big words. Instead, learn to build on these basics to allow your photographs to get better and better.

Aperture

Just like the iris in our eyes, the aperture is the adjustable opening in a camera, the size of which is controlled by a series of movable discs. (Aperture should not to be confused with shutter speed, discussed next, which is the length of time light is allowed into the camera). Aperture is measured by *f*-stops, and is written with a corresponding number, like *f*/5.6. A wide (or large) aperture allows more light into the camera and has a smaller *f*-stop number, while a narrow (or small) aperture allows less light into the camera and has a larger *f*-stop number. This can get confusing because it seems like the opposite should be true, but just to make things clear, here's an example: *f*/1.8 is considered a wide aperture, and *f*/32 is considered a very narrow one. On your camera, the aperture will usually be displayed on your LCD screen when you are composing your image. On more advanced cameras, look for the displayed aperture on the viewfinder. You will either see the *f*-stop displayed as *f*/1.8, *f*/1.8, or sometimes just 1.8—where 1.8 can be any aperture value.

Varying apertures can produce very different effects. With a wide aperture, the photograph will have a very shallow depth of field (DOF), the DOF being the part of the image that is in focus from front to back or near to far. With a shallow DOF, a subject is isolated from the rest of the image and the background. This is important when you really want the focus of the image to be the subject you're photographing, not the background. With a narrow aperture, there's a large DOF, meaning that most of the image will be in focus—just like when you squint your eyes. This is useful for landscapes or other images where you want everything in the frame to appear sharp.

1001, Daniel Platt (torteloni), age 16, Berlin, Germany
This shot is an example of a large depth of field; the entire frame is in focus, and even the tree at the farthest point appears sharp.
Kodak EasyShare C433
PHOTO © DANIEL PLATT

We Set Up the Trains, Dale Rothenberg (Pianisimo), age 16, Connecticut, USA
A perfect example of shallow depth of field: Only the toy train is in focus in this image.
Nikon D50, 50mm lens, ISO 1600, 1/60 sec. at *f*/1.8
PHOTO © DALE ROTHENBERG

Shutter Speed

The shutter speed indicates the amount of time the shutter—the device that allows light into the camera—is held open while you're taking a picture so that light can reach the film (in a traditional camera) or image sensor (in a digital camera). Shutter speed is not to be confused with aperture. Instead, think of it as a curtain that opens for varying lengths of time to allow light to pass through the aperture (or iris). Shutter speed is measured in seconds, and is written as a fraction. For example, a typical shutter speed for photographs taken in sunlight is 1/125 of a second.

In combination with various settings of the lens aperture, shutter speed regulates how much light the camera records. For any given exposure, a fast shutter speed needs a larger aperture (or more light), or your photo will end up underexposed. A slow shutter speed needs a smaller aperture, or your photo will be overexposed. Slow shutter speeds are usually used in low-light conditions, such as at night (see pages 44 and 70).

As with apertures, varying shutter speeds can be used to create different effects. For example, in sports photography, a photographer can use a fast shutter speed to freeze fast moving action. Slow shutter speeds, on the other hand, can be used to blur motion, such as the flowing water of a waterfall. Learning how to choose your shutter speed to create a certain effect takes practice, but can lead to compelling, unique imagery.

Tyler Czop, Switch Heelflip, Sean Dalin (sean dalin), age 19, British Columbia, Canada
A fast shutter speed is necessary to freeze rapidly moving action, such as in this shot of Tyler Czop doing a switch heelflip at the Chilliwack skate park in British Columbia.
Canon EOS 20D, 50mm lens, ISO 100, 1/640 sec. at f/1.8, Canon Speedlite 430EX flash
PHOTO © SEAN DALIN

Distraction (formerly *Love in Lights*), Patricia Gorospe Ramos (littlemisspatricia), age 14, Quezon City, Philippines
Slow shutter speeds can also be used to capture light trails. Try setting your camera up on a tripod, and use a pen light or glow stick to "draw" a design in the air; your camera will capture the strokes.
Canon EOS Digital Rebel XTi (400D), 18–55mm lens, ISO 400, 2 sec. at f/5.6, no flash F3.5–5.6 lens
PHOTO © PATRICIA GOROSPE RAMOS

Slow Shutter Scenery, Chris Stevens (chris17nz), age 17, Dunedin, New Zealand
A slow shutter speed was used to capture this wave breaking on rocks at Potato Point Surf Spot in New Zealand.
Canon EOS Digital Rebel XTi (400D), 18–55mm lens, tripod and remote shutter release, ISO 100, 4 sec. at f/11, no flash
PHOTO © CHRIS STEVENS

Film Speed (ISO/ASA)

Whether you're shooting film or digital, you will see the letters ISO (International Standards Organization) or ASA (American Standard Association) with a corresponding number either on the film package or on the camera itself. (On most cameras you can look for the ISO button and press it to view the actual number settings.) These letters and numbers refer to the film speed, or how sensitively the film or digital sensor reacts to light. Slower film speeds (low ISO numbers) indicate less sensitivity to light, so they generally require longer shutter speeds and/or wider (or larger) apertures; faster film speeds (high ISO numbers) indicate more light sensitivity, which means they are ideal for faster shutter speeds and smaller (narrower) apertures.

As a general rule (and this applies to both digital cameras and film cameras), you get a better quality image with a lower ISO. So if you are mostly taking pictures where there is sufficient available light, such as an outdoor portrait on a sunny day, setting your camera to the lowest possible ISO—ISO 50, for example—will give you the best image the camera is capable of.

If you want to take pictures in low light, such as a night portrait, you will need to supplement the existing light with a flash or other light source in order to be able to use a low ISO setting. While you can select a higher ISO to compensate for the lack of light in the scene, you risk the appearance of noise, or graininess, in your shot.

"Noise" is when you see specks of color in an image where there shouldn't be any. Let's say you photographed a beautiful white cloud, but instead of it looking like the clean, white cotton ball it should look like, you notice spots of pink, purple, and other colors all over it. These spots are what photographers call noise.

Noise can be eliminated, or at least be less obvious, by using a camera with a large image sensor (the mechanism inside all digital cameras that records the image). Ultimately, the size of an image sensor determines the ISO speed range that can be used to shoot a photograph without having the image suffer from undue noise. Most consumer point-and-shoot cameras have small image sensors; this allows them to fit into your pocket, but also means that noise will be more of a problem when shooting at high ISOs. Conversely, higher-end digital SLR (DSLR) cameras have larger image sensors, so noise is rarely a problem. But these cameras are less portable, more expensive, and not as easy to use as their more compact counterparts. You just need to weigh what qualities are most important to you.

Exposure

Now that you've learned the terms *aperture, shutter speed,* and *film speed*, it's time to learn why they are so important. You may have to read this section a few times to really get it, but that's okay. It's like riding a bicycle. Once you learn, you have the skills to move on your own.

Aperture, shutter speed, and film speed are the three elements that combine to create an exposure. And perhaps the most crucial lesson you'll ever need to master in order to take great pictures is the relationships among these three elements, and how to adjust each for the particular image you are trying to shoot.

Think of aperture, shutter speed, and film speed as three sliders on a sliding scale—move one too much and you tip the scale in one direction. The key is knowing exactly what you want to achieve and controlling each slider accordingly.

Let's say you want to photograph your flowers outside on a sunny day. The following settings will give you almost the same exposure values (amount of light hitting the photographic medium based on the shutter speed and aperture values):

1. Aperture *f*/28, shutter speed 1/100 sec. at ISO 100.
2. Aperture *f*/8, shutter speed 1/200 sec. at ISO 100.
3. Aperture *f*/22, shutter speed 1/25 sec. at ISO 100.

However, as you can see from the photos to the right, the pictures look different.

So how do you know which combination to pick? You learned that a lower ISO reduces the risk of noise and is the ideal choice if we have sufficient light, so pretend you decided on ISO 100 for that. What other questions do you need to ask yourself?

Do you want shallow depth of field so that your subject is isolated from the rest of the image (i.e., for the background to be blurred)? Then a large aperture of *f*/2.8 is for you. And since you know that a wider aperture needs a faster shutter speed to let light in for a briefer amount of time in order to prevent your image from over-exposure, then the combination in photo number 1 wins.

But what if you want more of the image to be in focus? You learned that a smaller aperture will give you a

1. Aperture f/2.8, shutter speed 1/1000 sec. at ISO 100

2. Aperture f/8, shutter speed 1/200 sec. at ISO 100

3. Aperture f/22, shutter speed 1/25 sec. at ISO 100

Exposure Shots, Charlie Styr (CharlieStyr), age 17, England, UK
These three shots have almost exactly the same exposure value, but as
the photos show, the resulting pictures look different.
Canon EOS Digital Rebel XTi (400D), 90mm lens
PHOTO © CHARLIE STYR

greater depth of field, so of all the choices listed above, f/22 would be the aperture setting to choose when you want most of your image in focus. Consequently, you would need a slower shutter speed to allow more light to pass through the smaller aperture to avoid underexposure, in which case the combination in photo number 3 is the most appropriate choice.

Looking for something in between? Then combination 2 is the one for you. If you can follow the logic above, let's take it one step further. The subject in this image is still, but if it were moving, then maybe capturing the motion would be more of a priority than depth of field, in which case you would use a faster shutter speed to freeze fast-moving action, choose a larger aperture to avoid underexposure, and select a low ISO if the light is inadequate. If you wanted to blur that moving subject, then you would use a slower shutter speed, choose a smaller aperture to avoid overexposure, and select a low ISO if there's enough light.

Remember, these are general guidelines: There are no concrete rules. You will have to play around with adjusting the settings to really understand the relationship among these three elements. With enough practice, you will master the art of choosing the winning combination for any given situation.

Recipe for a Picture

Photography is a creative process—but there are some guidelines that most photographers stick to when setting up a shot. Composition and lighting are two essential elements to consider when taking pictures. Learn to use them to your advantage.

Composition

The composition of an image refers to how you position your subject in the frame. There are no strict rules to composing an image, and it's something that is fun to experiment with. However, a general guideline taught in most "Photo 101" classes is the rule of thirds.

Imagine the frame in your viewfinder or LCD screen is divided equally into three parts, both vertically and horizontally, leaving a frame divided into nine rectangles to form a grid (shown below):

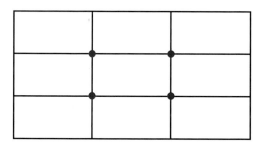

Most people's first instinct is to place the main point of focus right in the center (the middle rectangle). But instead, try placing it at any one of the four points where these lines intersect (see the red dots, above). This can create a more compelling photograph. For landscape photos especially, it often makes for a well-balanced image to line up your foreground, middle ground, and background with the horizontal lines running across the frame. A rule-of-thirds grid is built into some digital cameras, and can be turned on and viewed on the LCD screen, thereby allowing you to experiment with it.

Woodpigeon on Powerpole, Chris Stevens (chris17nz), age 17, Dunedin, New Zealand
If you were to place the grid onto this image of a pigeon silhouetted on a power line in Purakanui, New Zealand, you would see that the pigeon sits right where two lines on the bottom right intersect, making it a powerful focal point.
Canon EOS Digital Rebel XTi (400D), 18–55mm lens, ISO 200, 1/500 sec. at f/20, no flash
PHOTO © CHRIS STEVENS

Butterfly Dress, Hanah An (i am a mermaid princess.), age 17, New South Wales, Australia
In this self-portrait, Hanah posed within the right third of the frame, which resulted in a less predictable composition than if she had stood right in the middle.
Nikon D80, 18–135mm lens, tripod and remote shutter release, ISO 1000, 1/40 sec. at f/3.5
PHOTO © HANAH AN

Lighting

On the most basic level, the way you light your subject will determine how clearly you can see it in the final shot. At the creative level, how you use light can completely alter the look, mood, and overall impact of your image.

There are two main types of light to consider when shooting: natural light and artificial light. Natural (or ambient) light is the light that already exists in the scene you are shooting—the sunlight streaming into a room through the window or the dim light from streetlamps on an empty road. When you shoot using natural light, you shoot the scene as is, without an additional light source. The advantage of shooting in natural light is obvious in the very word used to describe it: natural. Capturing the scene as it exists creates a more natural re-creation of the scene for anyone viewing your image.

If you use an additional light source—a flash, strobe, even a flashlight or desk lamp—then you are shooting in artificial light, which opens up a whole new world of experimentation. If you like to set up your shots, you will have a lot of fun testing out how different light sources affect the final image. For example, if you are shooting a portrait, aiming light at your subject from different angles allows you to light up certain parts of the face, adding depth and shadows and creating a more dramatic image.

If shadows are something you want to avoid, whether you're shooting in natural or artificial light, one helpful tool is a reflector. You know how when you hold a mirror up to sunlight the light bounces off the reflective surface, creating a visible beam of light that will move as you move your mirror? Reflectors work the same way. They are used to bounce or redirect any existing light to areas in the scene or subject that are dark, to fill in the shadows with light. You can buy reflectors at any photo store, or

Weightless & Light, Hanah An (i am a mermaid princess.), age 17, New South Wales, Australia
Natural light from the window filters through these almost translucent clothes to create a soft, ethereal look.
Nikon D80, 18–135mm lens, ISO 320, 1/1000 sec. at f/5.6
PHOTO © HANAH AN

make your own by cutting a piece of white or even light gray posterboard to any size you want. Keep in mind that the bigger the board, the more light it will be able to catch and bounce. No posterboard in sight? Wrapping some tinfoil around a piece of cardboard also does the trick.

We'll get into specifics later—for indoor lighting, see page 36; for shooting in harsh daylight, see page 40; for shooting at night, see page 44 and 70; and for adjusting white balance (another way to make sure the light is not affecting how the color is rendered in your photograph), see page 83.

Apple Shower, Joshua Rozad (jbr_jbr), age 15, Ontario, Canada
The built-in flash was used to illuminate the splashes of water on this apple, photographed against a white piece of paper, to create a more vibrant image.
Canon PowerShot S3IS, tripod, ISO 80, 1/250 sec. at f/2.7, on-camera flash
PHOTO © JOSHUA ROZAD

A NOTE ABOUT POST-PROCESSING:

Many of the photos throughout this book have been altered, or "post-processed," on a computer using Photoshop or other image-editing software programs. Image-editing can be a great way to enhance your photographs. Some common image enhancements—all discussed in depth on pages 120 to 127—include cropping or cutting off unwanted parts of an image, such as too much sky on the upper third of your frame, to reshape it and create a more compelling shot; slightly sharpening parts of an image that are a bit blurry or out of focus; and adjusting the brightness or color of an image. Image enhancement allows you to tweak an image so that it better matches what you saw at the time you shot it. Often the image looks so realistic that it can be hard to tell if it has been enhanced.

Although some of the same computer programs used for *image enhancement* can also be used for another type of post-processing called *digital manipulation*, the two terms should not be confused. Digital manipulation is used to create a completely different image, maybe even a scene that could never exist in the real world. When you look at an image you can usually tell if it has been manipulated. As you will see on pages 129 to 131, digital manipulation allows you to do many creative, fun things with your pictures once you have taken them.

PEOPLE GET READY
PORTRAIT PHOTOGRAPHY

2

The world of portrait photography is huge—and encompasses topics you might not even immediately think of as portraiture. However, one thing that all portrait photography has in common is that it must have a subject. This chapter has essential information on taking some of the most popular types of portraits—from self-portraits to group shots to pet photographs. There are also technical tips on things you need to think about when you set up both outdoor and indoor shots.

Pensive in Thought, Hanah An (i am a mermaid princess.), age 17, New South Wales, Australia
Nikon D80, 18–135mm lens, ISO 320, 1/25 sec. at f/5.3, no flash
PHOTO © HANAH AN

Point of Interest
Isolating Your Subject

***Gotcha!*, Elisabeth Scheving (Eden Photography), age 19, Minnesota, USA**
A shallow depth of field allows the young girl's face to be in focus, isolating her from both the blurred foreground and the background.
Canon EOS 30D, 18–55mm lens, ISO 125, 1/50 sec. at f/4.5, no flash
PHOTO © EDEN PHOTOGRAPHY

PRO TIP
Use selective focus to drive the viewer's attention to the most important element of the composition. Selective focus can be obtained by using the widest aperture available.

JIM ERICKSON

One essential part of taking a portrait is isolating your subject, or setting him or her apart from the background. When your subject is isolated, your portrait is more powerful because viewers are not distracted by what is happening in the background.

The key to isolating your subject is knowing how to adjust your aperture. By using a wide aperture (small *f*-stop), you can get a very shallow depth of field, blurring the background and isolating your subject in the frame. An easy way to do this is by using the built-in portrait setting found in most compact cameras. Look for a button showing a silhouette or a portrait option in the settings menu. Selecting Portrait mode will force the camera to use the widest aperture possible and automatically isolate the subject for you.

On SLRs and more advanced cameras, use the Aperture Priority mode to select the widest aperture possible, which is normally around f/2.8 or f/3.5 at the lens's widest setting. (As you zoom in, you will find that the maximum aperture will decrease to f/5.6 or f/6.3.)

With a shallow depth of field, not all of your subject's face may be in focus, so it's important to choose a main point of focus. I personally find that a person's eyes reveal the most emotion and character, and I want them to appear sharp in the image, so I tend to focus on them. The mouth is another good point to zero in on. Experiment with different points—you will learn to create unique portraits that are much more eye-catching than typical head-and-shoulder shots.

You will most likely encounter two focus options—autofocus, in which the camera automatically selects a point of focus for you depending on how you frame the shot, and manual focus, in which you control which point you want the camera to hone in on.

The easiest way to focus in on your subject's eyes (or whichever point you've chosen) is to do it yourself using manual focus. If you have a compact camera, look for an option in the settings menu that lets you switch to manual focus. On more advanced cameras, there may be a switch and focusing ring on the lens that you spin to adjust your focus. Look in the viewfinder and adjust the focus until you target the sharpest point in the frame (in this case, the eyes).

Disturbed, Joshua Beam (Josh Beam), age 15, Texas, USA
A shallow depth of field can add drama to a shot, as in this photo of a young boy in Woodlands, Texas; his nose and right eye are the main point of focus, while the rest of his face is in shadow.
Pentax K110D, 18–55mm lens, ISO 200, 1/30 sec. at f/4.5, no flash
PHOTO © JOSHUA BEAM

Prom Queen, Sarah Lee (Sarah Lee), age 17, Hawaii, USA
Using an on-camera flash in a low-light situation is another way to isolate your subject, such as in this senior prom portrait.
Canon EOS Digital Rebel XT (350D), 50mm lens, ISO 100, 2/5 sec. at f/1.8, Canon Speedlite 530EX flash
PHOTO © SARAH LEE

Just because the background is blurred doesn't mean it's not an important part of the picture. A simple studio photography trick is to place your subject in front of a plain white, black, or gray background. Or, if you want to make your subject really pop out, play around with colored backgrounds that contrast with what he or she is wearing. If your subject is wearing a green shirt, for example, place her in front of a pink or red wall and the image will have lots of energy.

You can also try an outdoor location or somewhere with lights behind your subject. When you use a wide aperture, highlights that are out of focus appear as disks of light, giving an interesting, almost surreal background glow to the shot. The photographic term for this look is *bokeh* (pronounced boke-aay), which comes from the Japanese word bokeaji, meaning blur.

Note that backgrounds don't always have to be blurred out. In an "environmental portrait," for example, the background plays a huge role in revealing something extra about your subject. For more on that type of image, see page 32.

Exit Only, Sean Dalin (sean dalin), age 19, British Columbia, Canada
Instead of using a shallow depth of field, you can use a colored
background to isolate your subject.
Canon EOS 20D, 18–55mm lens, ISO 100, 1/250 sec. at f/4, Canon Speedlite 430EX flash
PHOTO © SEAN DALIN

Wait, Susannah Benjamin (ireland1324), age 14, Connecticut, USA
Take a more unique approach to portraiture by focusing on something instead of your subject's face. This subject's chipped nail polish and the cracks on the post add texture to the shot.
Nikon D80, 18–135mm lens, ISO 200, 1/320 sec. at f/4.5, no flash

In the Wheat Field, Joshua Rozad (jbr_jbr), age 15, Ontario, Canada
In this example of shallow depth of field, the monotoned wheat in the foreground and background of this frame isolates the subject's face even more.
Canon PowerShot S3IS, ISO 80, 1/800 sec. at f/2.7, no flash

What Goes Where
Composing a Portrait

Refuge, Susannah Benjamin (ireland1324), age 14, Connecticut, USA
Get close up and focus on the eyes to create a sense of intimacy
between your subject and the viewer.
Nikon D80, 18–135mm lens, ISO 200, 1/60 sec. at f/5, no flash
PHOTO © SUSANNAH BENJAMIN

PRO TIP
Give your pictures an attitude. Get high. Get low.
Roll around on the ground—whatever it might
take to discover a different point of view.
MATTHEW WAKEM

While the rule of thirds (page 20) is the best guideline for
composing any shot, the orientation of your portrait—
whether the image is vertical or horizontal—is another
thing to think about. There are also big decisions to make,
such as what angle to shoot from and what to include in
the frame.

There is a reason that shots taken vertically are
referred to as being in "portrait" orientation: the human
face fits much better in a vertical frame. However, you can
also take portraits horizontally, in "landscape" orientation,
especially when you want more of the background in a shot.
Using landscape orientation can lead to unpredictable,
interesting portraits, and is especially effective for

An Emerald Gaze, Elisabeth Scheving (Eden Photography), age 19, Minnesota, USA
This senior portrait takes a common portrait composition—a head-and-shoulders shot photographed using a portrait orientation—and adds interest by shooting from above.
Canon EOS 30D, 17–85mm lens, ISO 125, 1/1250 sec. at f/1.8, no flash
PHOTO © EDEN PHOTOGRAPHY

environmental portraits, which intentionally include the subject's surroundings.

The angle you use and the way your subject is posed also play major roles in your portrait. For your standard head-and-shoulders shot, angle the camera at eye level, directly in front of your subject so that he or she is looking straight into the lens. This is a pretty straightforward way of shooting a portrait, and while it's effective, you might want to experiment with shots that are less predictable—like a portrait that shows just the profile of a subject, or part of the face, or maybe one that doesn't even show the face at all.

If someone has asked you to shoot his or her portrait, take time beforehand to look at examples of ways to compose the shot so that you come prepared and your portrait session can be more spontaneous. Look at the photographs of famous portraitists like Arnold Newman, Richard Avedon, Annie Leibovitz, Irving Penn, and Martin Schoeller. What do you like about the angles they used or how they posed their subjects? When you know what you want, you can more easily direct your subject to portray that look.

Open Up Your Eyes, Liel Bomberg (Liel Bomberg), age 16, Petah Tikva, Israel
Squat down on the ground. Shooting from below makes your subject appear taller, and in this case, emphasizes the upward toss of the bouquet.
Canon PowerShot A720IS, ISO 80, 1/640 sec. at f/4, no flash
PHOTO © LIEL BOMBERG

Pathway to Summer, Elisabeth Scheving (Eden Photography), age 19, Minnesota, USA

A landscape orientation reveals more of the environment the subject was photographed in, adding a sense of place.

Kodak EasyShare C330, ISO 80, 1/500 sec. at f/5.1, no flash

:PHOTO © EDEN PHOTOGRAPHY

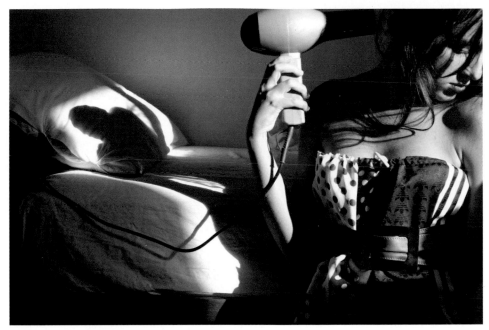

My Hairdryer Can Shoot, Claudia Attaianese (principear*), age 17, Naples, Italy
By using a landscape orientation and placing the subject in the right third of
the frame, you can create a less predictable composition.
Canon EOS Digital Rebel (300D), 18–55mm lens, ISO 100, 1/100 sec. at f/7.1, no flash
PHOTO © CLAUDIA ATTAIANESE

Dandelion Silhouette, Joshua Rozad (jbr_jbr), age 15, Ontario, Canada
Be original. You can show just the subject's profile, or maybe none of the face at all.
Canon PowerShot S3IS, tripod, ISO 80, 1/1250 sec. at f/2.7, no flash
PHOTO © JOSHUA ROZAD

Who's That Girl (or Boy)?
Revealing Your Subject's Character

Modern Nymph, Susannah Benjamin (ireland1324), age 14, Connecticut, USA
Composing the shot in a unique way can reveal a subject's quirky side.
Nikon D80, 18–135mm lens, ISO 400, 1/60 sec. at f/4, on-camera flash
PHOTO © SUSANNAH BENJAMIN

PRO TIP
When photographing someone who seems self-conscious, take a few frames and wander off to give your subject a break. Repeat this two or three times, and the subject will grow comfortable and often enjoy the process.
PIERRE CROCQUET

A successful portrait captures the essence of your subject, providing a glimpse into his or her true character. If you're thinking of shooting someone's portrait, start by asking yourself questions about your subject: What does she do for a living? Does he have any special hobbies or interests? What do most people think about when they think about this person? Once you have answered these questions, think about what parts of that person's identity you want to call attention to, and how you can use elements like props, location, clothing, and posing to help reveal those qualities.

A prop is most effective when it immediately shows viewers something they wouldn't know just by looking at the subject. For example, if your subject loves music, shoot

Put a Record On, by Stephen McLeod Blythe
(StephenMcleod), age 19, Glasgow, Scotland
In this portrait the headphones and the
girl's expression and pose immediately
convey her interest in music.
Canon EOS Digital Rebel XT (350D), ISO 100, 1/100
sec. at f/10, two Jessops Portaflash flashes
PHOTO © STEPHEN MCLEOD BLYTHE

a picture of him or her wearing headphones or playing guitar. Even better, use a combination of props and location. So if your music-loving subject is part of a band, take his or her portrait—favorite instrument in hand—on stage or in a recording studio. Show that your subject is a serious student by seating him behind stacks of books in a library. If the person you are photographing loves cars, photograph him behind the wheel of his car or in a parking lot standing next to it.

This type of photograph is called an environmental portrait, and you'll often see contemporary professional photographers use this method when shooting a famous actress on the set of her latest film or a businessman sitting in his grand office surrounded by city views.

In addition to location and props, the way your subject is posed can also say a lot about his or her personality. Generally, someone who is looking directly at the camera and laughing in a natural way will seem like a confident person, while someone who is looking down, hiding his or her eyes, and smiling coyly is probably on the shy side.

Oh Dear, Stephen McLeod Blythe (StephenMcleod), age 19, Glasgow, Scotland
This humorous portrait of a band member taking a break during a
recording session shows how location can be used to reveal something
about your subject's character.
Canon EOS 5D, 50mm lens, ISO 1600, 1/125 sec. at f/4, on-camera flash
PHOTO © STEPHEN MCLEOD BLYTHE

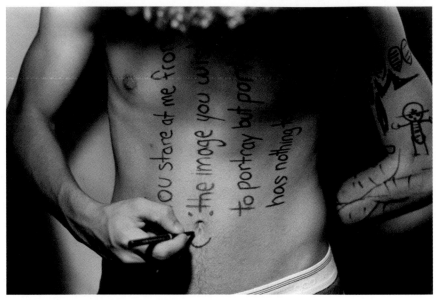

Dave, Mathea Millman (midnight zara), age 16, New York, USA
You don't always need to show a subject's face to portray his character; instead, create a telling mood using lighting, composition, and posing.
Nikon 8008 AF (film)
PHOTO © MATHEA MILLMAN

Chipped Teeth, Sean Dalin (sean dalin), age 19, British Columbia, Canada
Think of something your subject is interested in and use a combination of clothing and props to reveal that part of his personality.
Canon EOS 20D, 10–22mm lens, ISO 100, 1/250 sec. at f/4, Canon Speedlite 430EX flash
PHOTO © SEAN DALIN

Licks of Love, Elisabeth Scheving
(Eden Photography), age 19,
Minnesota, USA

Shooting a portrait from a distance
can make the image seem more
candid, as if you're capturing your
subject in a private moment.
Canon EOS 30D, 17–85mm lens, ISO 100,
1/320 sec. at f/2, no flash

Beautiful on the Inside
Photographing People Indoors

The World Is Passing Us By, Ben Shapiro (shap43), age 19, New York, USA
By raising your ISO in a low-light situation like this one, you will increase
your digital image sensor's sensitivity to the existing light in a scene.
Canon EOS 20D, 50mm lens, no flash
PHOTO © BEN SHAPIRO

PRO TIP

When you're learning how to light a subject for a
photograph, it's best to begin with one light at a
time. Concentrate on what you're looking for with
that one light first, and you'll have the best
control over your results.

F. SCOTT SCHAFER

Getting crisp images indoors can be a challenge when
little light is available, but there are two main ways to
overcome this. The most obvious solution is to use a flash.
A flash is an easy fix, and you will find that if you leave a
camera in auto mode, it will almost always trigger the flash
in a low-light situation. The flash lights up your subject
and creates a situation where a higher shutter speed is
needed to expose the image correctly, creating a crisp,
high-contrast image.

There are some disadvantages to using a flash. First,
it will more than likely illuminate only your subject,

leaving the background in the dark. Also, if you are capturing a subject from a distance, the light from the flash may not reach it.

In situations like these, your other option is to raise the ISO, or light sensitivity (of the sensor in your digital camera), to allow for more light to be captured. Raise the ISO by simply increasing the number of the ISO setting on your camera. (Refer to your manual to find out how.) Just as with a flash, increasing your ISO will allow you to use higher shutter speeds, resulting in equally crisp shots. The advantage of using this method rather than a flash is that it will create a more realistic image. The entire picture will be exposed the same way, and the shot will be more like what you are seeing with your own eyes. This technique is more effective than flash when you want to capture an entire scene—like a group shot of your friends dancing at a party—and not just one subject.

By increasing your ISO and using a flash at the same time, your foreground will be lit up by the flash and the detail in the background will also be seen. This may sound like the best option of all, but only trial and error will show if this is the effect you want.

Of course, you won't always need to use a flash when shooting portraits indoors. Natural light can provide incredible mood and effect. Sunlight filtering through a window can flood a room with more than enough light. You can then use reflectors to direct that light onto the various parts of your subject, like his or her face, for example, that need more illumination (see page 41 for more on reflectors). If you're feeling really creative, try positioning lamps or flashlights in strategic places around your subject—such as from behind as a backlight, for example—mimicking a professional studio setup. This will help you understand how light affects the mood of an image, and to better control light to get the portrait you want. A tripod is also a helpful addition to any portrait setup when you need to keep the camera steady in one position for prolonged periods of time.

Beauty, Joshua Rozad (jbr_jbr), age 15, Ontario, Canada
Position your subject in front of a bright lamp or window to illuminate his or her face and create catchlight—the slight sparkle in a subject's eyes.
Nikon D40x, 55–200mm lens, tripod, ISO 400, 1/20 sec. at f/5.6, no flash, black backdrop
PHOTO © JOSHUA ROZAD

You Talkin' to Me?, Anton Edvard Kristensen (Anton Edvard Kristensen), age 16, Reykjavík, Iceland
In this self-portrait, a homemade softbox (standalone light enclosed with translucent material) is used to diffuse light and create a less harsh lighting situation.
Canon EOS Digital Rebel XTi (400D), 18–55mm lens, ISO 100, 1/200 sec. at f/5.6, homemade softbox
PHOTO © ANTON EDVARD KRISTENSEN

Magic, Jamie Ringoen (jamie.marie), age 16, Colorado, USA

Try positioning light sources, like a lamp or flashlight, in strategic spots—such as behind and in front of your subject—and shoot the image without flash for dramatic effect.

Canon EOS 60D, ISO 100, 1/40 sec. at f/0, no flash

PHOTO © JAMIE RINGOEN

The Sound of White, Hanah An (i am a mermaid princess.),
age 17, New South Wales, Australia
Even indoors, you can use natural (existing) light to
your advantage and shoot a portrait without flash.
Nikon D80, 18–135mm lens, tripod and remote shutter release,
ISO 1000, 1/80 sec. at f/4.5, no flash
PHOTO © HANAH AN

The Sound of Longing, Sean Dalin (sean dalin), age 19, British Columbia, Canada
Light draws the eye, giving that part of the image extra importance. Here, the photographer
makes a connection between the microphone and the musician by using light to draw your
eye to both. The musician is illuminated with natural light pouring in through the window,
while the microphone is lit it with the clean, white light of a flash.
Canon EOS 20D, 10–22mm lens, ISO 100, 1/250 sec. at f/4.5, Canon Speedlite 430EX flash
PHOTO © SEAN DALIN

Under the Sun
Taking Outdoor Portraits in Daylight

By the Seaside, I Want to Go, Hanah An (i am a mermaid princess.), age 17, New South Wales, Australia

To shoot a portrait outside on a sunny day, avoid harsh shadows by finding a spot for your subject where there's no (or not much) direct sun hitting her face. There should also be light *behind you*. In other words, don't stand under a tree or in shade to take the photo. This way, there will still be indirect light bouncing off your subject's face.

Nikon D80, 18–135mm lens, ISO 200, 1/400 sec. at f/5, no flash

PHOTO © HANAH AN

PRO TIP

Never underestimate the power of natural light, and how you can work even the smallest bit of daylight with a reflector in a difficult lighting situation.

SARA REMINGTON

Taking outdoor portraits during the day has its own set of challenges, mostly involving light. When you shoot in peak sunlight—usually between noon and 2:00 P.M.—you have to deal with harsh shadows on your subject's face. They may look like normal shadows when you are taking the picture, but a careful look at the final image may shock you. Harsh shadows tend to make the subject's eyes appear dark, and the shadow under the nose exaggerates its size—not something many subjects would find flattering.

One way to avoid this problem is by waiting for a cloudy day. A lot of people think an overcast sky is not ideal for outdoor photography, but it actually offers the best lighting conditions. Clouds diffuse light evenly over

Travis, Sean Dalin (sean dalin), age 19, British Columbia, Canada
Choose a time of day when the light is not so harsh—early morning or late afternoon.
Canon EOS 20D, 18–55mm lens, ISO 100,1/1000 sec. at f/4, no flash
PHOTO © SEAN DALIN

the earth's surface, so your photos won't have harsh shadows—and your subject can retain the look of his or her original nose. You can also shoot in the shade, where it will still be fairly bright, but again without harsh, direct light. Shooting under a tree that's in direct sunlight, for example, can create an interesting, dappled effect.

If none of these are options, here is another fix for harsh shadows: fill flash. A fill flash is a small burst from your camera's flash that mixes with natural light to fill in the dark spots on your subject's face, removing harsh shadows. To do this on SLRs and cameras with pop-up flashes, you simply pop up the flash and it will happen

automatically. On compact cameras, look for a button with a lightning bolt or the word *flash*, and press it to tell the camera that you want to enable the flash, even though it is bright. Once you have enabled the flash, take the portrait as you would normally and the final image should have no facial shadows.

Another simple alternative is to use a reflector. If you don't have one handy, use a piece of white or silver posterboard, available at most art supply stores. Use the board to reflect existing light back onto your subject, helping to eliminate any shadows and putting a sparkle in his or her eyes.

Overcast days are actually the best time to take outdoor photos. Clouds act as natural softboxes, diffusing light and creating a gentle lighting situation that's ideal for outdoor portraits. Notice how all three of these photos have no harsh shadows.

Cambridge Cobbles, Susannah Benjamin (ireland1324), age 14, Connecticut, USA
Nikon D80, 18–135mm lens, ISO 180, 1/500 sec. at f/3.8
PHOTO © SUSANNAH BENJAMIN

Fall Has…Fallen?, Jamie Ringoen (jamie.marie), age 16, Colorado, USA
Canon EOS 60D, 18mm lens, ISO 200, 1/800 sec. at f/0, no flash
PHOTO © JAMIE RINGOEN

Ajah, Elisabeth Scheving (Eden Photography), age 19, Minnesota, USA
Canon EOS 30D, 17–85mm lens, ISO 640, 1/4000 sec. at f/2, no flash
PHOTO © EDEN PHOTOGRAPHY

Superman, Hanah An (i am a mermaid princess.), age 17, New South Wales, Australia

If you can't avoid peak sunlight, improvise with interesting poses and angles to prevent shadows in your subject's face.

Nikon D00, 10–135mm lens, ISO 100, 1/200 sec. at f//.1, no flash

PHOTO © HANAH AN

A Shot in the Dark
Taking Outdoor Portraits at Night

***Night Lights*, Hanah An (i am a mermaid princess.), age 17,
New South Wales, Australia**
Use a long shutter speed and high ISO to capture existing light and
freeze movement, such as in this shot at the Sydney Opera House with
the lights of the harbor in the background.
Nikon D100, lens?, 1/20 sec. at f/2.8, no flash
PHOTO © HANAH AN

PRO TIP
Put gels (colored filters or cellophane) on your
light sources, whether it's your on-camera flash
or the lamp in your living room. A red or blue
gel can create a totally different mood.
MATTHEW WAKEM

Taking outdoor photographs of people at night is one of
the most difficult aspects of portraiture. The lower light
means you have to shoot at slower shutter speeds, and the
images have a tendency to blur. The most common solution
is to use a flash. Most new digital cameras also have a mode
called Night Portrait or Slow Sync Flash. Both of these
modes enable the camera to take a photograph using
flash, but then keep the shutter open after it has fired the
flash to allow any existing natural light into the camera,
too. This is the genius behind Slow Sync Flash; it combines
flash with a long exposure so that you get the illumination
of the subject, but also the details in the background, so it
doesn't look like your subject is standing in a black hole.

If you're using a point-and-shoot camera, the Night Portrait or Slow Sync Flash mode may be embedded in a menu within your camera settings options. If you're using a digital SLR, you can find it by looking for an icon of a person with a star behind them on the mode dial. Once you've found the mode and are ready to start taking pictures, just remember that you're dealing with slow shutter speeds. To get a good photograph, you need to keep the camera steady while capturing the shot, so it is advisable to use a tripod; if you don't have a tripod, improvise and find a stable, flat surface like a fence, ladder step, or stool on which you can rest your camera.

You can also use Slow Sync Flash mode for more artistic purposes, such as capturing a halo of motion blur around your subject, or to make her appear to be in multiple places at one time in the same frame. To do this, first set your camera on Slow Sync Flash mode. As soon as the flash has fired, tell your subject either to move quickly—nod her head, swing her arms—or to change position and then hold that position until the shutter is released (you'll hear a clicking sound). It may take a few tries to get the shot you want, but it's a very entertaining way to spend your time.

A common problem worth mentioning when using any kind of flash in portraits is red eye. Red eye is a photographic effect that usually occurs when you use a flash in a very dark room. The sudden burst of light while the subject's pupils are wide open causes the eyes to appear unnaturally red, much like you would imagine a devil's or other villain's eyes to look in a horror movie.

While you can, to some extent, fix red eye using imaging-editing software like Photoshop, it's a time-consuming process. A more time-efficient alternative is to prevent red eye from happening when taking the picture.

Many new cameras have a built-in red-eye reduction flash function. If you're not sure whether your camera has this feature, check the manual. It will tell you how to enable the function, which often involves triggering a pre-flash—or series of low-power flashes—that will cause the iris to contract, allowing the pupil enough time to close before the main flash fires.

If your camera doesn't have this function, you can still prevent red eye by increasing the existing light in the scene, for example, by bringing in other lights like lamps or flashlights and positioning them around the subject. The brighter the existing light in a scene before the flash fires, the fewer your chances of encountering the red-eye effect.

And Suddenly, I'm a Ghost, Adam R. Eckert (A. Eckert), age 19, Wisconsin, USA
Set your camera up on a tripod and try shooting at slow shutter speeds, like this image shot at 5 seconds (at f/8 at ISO 100) to capture more background detail.
Canon EOS Digital Rebel XTi (400D), 28–135mm lens, tripod, ISO 100, 5 sec. at f/8, no flash
PHOTO © ADAM R. ECKERT

Train Far Away From Home, Miles George Dixon (milesgeorgee), age 17, Lincolnshire, England
Turn off the autoflash function on your point-and-shoot camera and focus on the existing light instead of your subject to create a moody silhouette.
Canon PowerShot A400, 1/100 sec. at f/3.8, no flash
PHOTO © MILES GEORGE DIXON

Friends til the End, Sarah Lee (Sarah Lee), age 17, Hawaii, USA

Use flash for nighttime portraits to illuminate your subjects.
Canon EOS Digital Rebel XT (350D), 18–55mm lens, ISO 200, 1/40 sec. at ƒ/3.5,
on-camera flash

PHOTO © SARAH LEE

Perspective, Benjamin Ang Zhen Ming (nccair), age 18, Singapore, Singapore

If there is enough light for you to see your subject's face in front of you, try turning off the autoflash function of your point-and-shoot. This allows you to capture more of the existing light from windows and streetlamps.

Canon PowerShot S5IS, ISO 200, 8 sec. at f/2.7, no flash

PHOTO © BENJAMIN ANG ZHEN MING

Shopping Cart Ollies, Sean Dalin (sean dalin), age 19, British Columbia, Canada

Keep in mind that a flash will illuminate a scene only up to about 16 feet (5 meters)—just enough to capture Richie Frisson skateboarding in a parking lot in Chilliwack, British Columbia.

Canon EOS 20D, 18–55mm lens, ISO 400, 1/50 sec. at f/4.5, Canon Speedlite 430EX flash

PHOTO © SEAN DALIN

A Photographer's Best Friend
Pet Shots

Beautiful Cat, Birkir Örn Björnsson (rikribsson), age 13, Reykjavik, Iceland
Photograph your pet in a shady spot outside, not only to create a more natural-looking portrait but also to avoid harsh shadows.
Samsung NV10, ISO 100, 1/500 sec. at f/2.8, no flash
PHOTO © BIRKIR ÖRN BJÖRNSSON

PRO TIP

Experiment, experiment, experiment. Digital cameras are revelatory in their instant feedback. Pan with a moving subject to create an impressionistic blur, play with quirky camera angles, and above all, have fun!

ART WOLFE

I have a dog, and I've tried to take its picture many times but without much success. One day, I was absolutely determined to get at least one good image of her and decided that our garden was the best location because it is her favorite place to play. While the final photograph was still not what I would consider a perfect shot, I did learn a thing or two from the experience.

A fundamental aspect of pet photography is patience. Your pet may be edgy around cameras, particularly cameras with loud shutters and autofocus; the noise can be confusing and slightly scary to animals. However, with a bit of time, your

Fetch, Charlie Styr (CharlieStyr), age 17, England, UK
Photograph your pet in a spot they feel comfortable, like your backyard.
Canon EOS Digital Rebel XTi (400D), 50mm lens, ISO 100, 1/320 sec. at f/6.3, no flash
PHOTO © CHARLIE STYR

pet will become accustomed to the noises and, as a result, be a more cooperative subject. If you take your pet to a place where it is comfortable, outside on its favorite patch of grass in your yard, for example, you will generally find that your pet will be calmer and easier to photograph.

Before you try to sit your pet down for a session, think about how you want the final photograph to look. Bringing out your pet's character in a photograph can be somewhat of a challenge. You might find it easier to include props. After all, a favorite toy may be all you need to bring out Fido's playful side. You may also choose not to sit your pet down at all, but to let it act as it normally does and simply wait for the perfect moment to click the shutter.

If your pet has a particularly interesting face, try a close-up that gives a full-frame view of every wrinkle, whisker, or colorful feather. Of course, getting your pet to actually look at the camera can prove challenging, as animals generally don't stop moving. Ask a friend or relative to try and hold your pet steady until you're ready to take the photo, or if your animal is trained, have some treats on hand as a reward for good behavior. I like to combine close-ups with full body shots, particularly for dogs and cats, so you can see the details of the coat and get an idea of how big the animal is.

Whether a close-up or from farther away, taking a picture of your pet from eye level is one of the most overlooked angles of pet photography. You should get down on the ground (or high above, depending on what kind of pet you have) so that your pet is face-to-face with the lens—it creates a more intimate and realistic portrait.

An outdoor shoot in a shady spot or on an overcast day is ideal because direct sunlight on your pet's coat can cause unnatural spots and colors in the final photograph. This is especially true if your pet's coat or feathers are both black and white—exposing for one color will cause the other to appear like a blob without any detail because the contrast range between the two colors is too wide. Shooting in the shade reduces the contrast. If you can't avoid the sun, you can also use fill flash as described in the previous essay, Under the Sun: Taking Outdoor Portraits in Daylight, on page 40.

Try to avoid using a flash, as animals' eyes are particularly susceptible to the red- or green-eye effect you see in photographs. If you must use a flash, apply the red-eye reduction tips discussed in the previous essay. But also be warned that a flash may cause an animal's coat (or feathers) to appear overly shiny and unappealing because an animal's coat tends to reflect light from the flash.

What if your friend is neither furry nor feathery but instead lives in a glass house? We'll tackle more tips for photographing creatures in an aquarium setting in Underwater Photography on page 86. For now, keep in mind that flashes and glass don't mix well naturally, so use existing light when you can, or try different angles to avoid getting glare from the flash in the final shot.

Goat, William A. Clark (thespacesuitcatalyst), age 16, California, USA
Try to photograph an animal at eye level in order to create
intimacy between the subject and the viewer.
Canon EOS Digital Rebel XT (350D), 50mm lens
PHOTO © WILLIAM A. CLARK

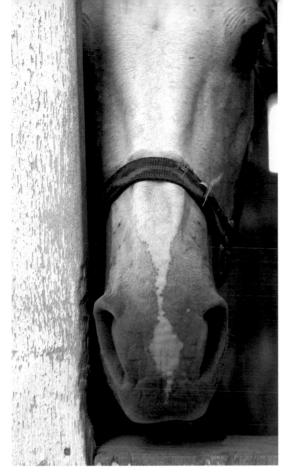

Rustic Wonder, Rachel Valenziano (RachelLyn), age 15, Nebraska, USA
Experiment with composition. In this shot, the horse's face takes up the entire two thirds of the frame, resulting in a more interesting image.
Canon EOS Digital Rebel XTi (400D), 50mm lens
PHOTO © RACHEL VALENZIANO

Pascal's Ball, Lauren Botteron (LBott), age 19, Missouri, USA
Incorporate your pet's favorite toy into the shot to capture his playful side.
Minolta Maxxum 5, Kodak T-MAX-100 film, self-processed in a darkroom.
PHOTO © LAUREN BOTTERON

Dove, Matt Sprague (mattspragoo), age 17, Maryland, USA
Photographing a bird from below against a bright blue sky can result in a dramatic silhouette.
Nikon D50, 50mm lens, ISO 400, 1/640 sec. at f/4.2, no flash
PHOTO © MATT SPRAGUE

Golden Hour, Sarah Lee (Sarah Lee), age 17, Hawaii, USA
Try to capture your pet in an interesting pose, like this face and paw shot of a tabby cat relaxing in the sunlight on a pair of faded jeans.
Canon EOS Digital Rebel XT (350D), 18–55mm lens, ISO 400, 1/125 sec. at f/7.1, no flash
PHOTO © SARAH LEE

Three's a Crowd
Taking Group Shots

Sing It Loud, Collin Hughes (Collin Hughes), age 20, **Minnesota, USA**
Previously mentioned portraiture tips, like using both existing light and a flash to illuminate your subject, also apply in a group setting.
Nikon D70, 18–70mm lens, tripod, ISO 800, 1/5 sec. at f/6.3, Nikon SB-600 AF Speedlight flash
PHOTO © COLLIN HUGHES

PRO TIP
Make sure you have good music on set.
It puts everybody at ease.
BEN WATTS

All the tips and techniques discussed throughout this section also apply to group portraits. Just like in solo shots, you want to isolate your subjects, reveal something about their character, and choose an interesting location or composition. The unique challenge of a group portrait is that you have to apply all these techniques to multiple subjects at the same time.

Depending on how many people you're photographing, and the various personalities involved, this can be a daunting task—especially since you want to make sure everyone is in the frame. The most important thing to remember is that you need the widest frame possible to fit everyone into the shot. This is where the advantage of

Fiddling, Jamie Ringoen
(jamie.marie), age 16,
Colorado, USA
Use props just as you
would in a solo portrait
to reveal more about the
group of people you're
photographing, such as
in this shot of three sisters playing their fiddles
on a hill.
Canon PowerShot A610, tripod
and self-timer, 1/1250 sec. at
f/4, no flash, converted to black
and white in Photoshop
PHOTO © JAMIE RINGOEN

advantage of using a digital camera comes in: You can use the screen as a viewfinder, instantly see what the picture will look like, and delete any less-than-great ones as you shoot.

When I think of the least creative type of group portrait, I imagine the class portraits taken in school, where everyone is lined up in straight rows, looking stiff and frozen. Often, the most interesting portraits result when people are not so perfectly posed. It's extra important to help the people feel comfortable with each other and in front of the camera. For example, if you are covering the cheerleading team at a sporting event, ask them to recite cheers and act out some moves as you click the shutter. Not everyone may be looking at the camera at the same time, but you're sure to chance upon some interesting shots.

One tip for shooting photos of groups is to use the Continuous Shooting mode. When this setting is on, you simply hold your finger down on the shutter button and the camera takes a number of frames in rapid succession. You can then look through them and delete all but the best. This is also a great way to capture your subjects in more spontaneous poses than when they are all standing frozen, smiling for their one big shot. Continuous Shooting mode is accessible through the menu settings on a compact point-and-shoot camera or via a dedicated Continuous Shooting button on a more advanced digital SLR. (See pages 75 and 93 for more on this function.)

A lot of newer digital cameras also have a function called "face detection," which can be helpful with group portraits. Face detection lets the camera decide when everyone is facing the camera with their eyes open, and then takes the picture for you. It works by looking for the triangle between the eyes and mouth and then focusing on it before clicking the shutter. It also monitors for when the subjects' eyes are closed and waits for them to open before taking the picture.

PRO TIP
When in doubt, shoot black and white.
Everyone loves it!
DIRK KIKSTRA

Waiting (black and white), Sarah Lee (Sarah Lee), age 17, Hawaii, USA
For a candid group portrait, avoid posing your subjects. Instead, ask your
subjects to act naturally; then use a slow shutter speed to blur any motion.
Canon EOS Digital Rebel XT (350D), 18–55mm lens, ISO 100, no flash

Dinner at the Kona Brewing Company, Sarah Lee (Sarah Lee), age 17, Hawaii, USA
When photographing big groups, like in this portrait of a girls' water polo team in Hawaii, it's useful to use the Continuous Shooting mode to take a rapid succession of shots. It can be hard to get everyone looking good, so it helps to have a number of shots to choose from.
Canon EOS Digital Rebel XT (350D), 18–55mm lens, ISO 400, 1/60 sec. at f/3.5, on-camera flash
@CRED:PHOTO © SARAH LEE

Waiting for the Bus, William A. Clark (thespacesuitcatalyst), age 16, California, USA
Try casually posing your subjects next to each other and use a landscape orientation for small groups, like in this portrait of the indie-folk band Candle.
Canon EOS Digital Rebel XT (350D), 50mm lens
PHOTO © WILLIAM A. CLARK

Sisters, Danica Cheetham (Danica Jade), age 16, Queensland, Australia
Play with poses and configurations to fit everyone in the frame while still creating an interesting composition.
Fujifilm FinePix S7000
PHOTO © DANICA CHEETHAM

It's All About Me
Taking Self-Portraits

Self-Portrait, Danica Cheetham (Danica Jade), age 16,
Queensland, Australia

If you don't have a tripod, rest your camera on a steady,
flat surface and pose in front of it instead.

Fujifilm FinePix S7000

PHOTO © DANICA CHEETHAM

PRO TIP

Shoot film. No one is going to look back at his
or her contact sheets in fifteen years and say,
"Gosh, I wish I had shot this on digital."

CHRIS BUCK

A self-portrait is much like a normal portrait, except that
you are both the photographer and the subject, which can
prove to be an interesting situation. From a technical
standpoint, it obviously means that you have to be in the
picture and take it at the same time. If you want to do this
without having to hold the camera at arm's length (which
can be tough, unless you have superlong arms), your new
best friend is the Self-Timer mode.

The Self-Timer mode is found on almost all cameras,
normally indicated with a stopwatch icon. Turn the Self-
Timer mode on, then rest your camera on a flat, steady
surface (or use a tripod). Make sure the camera is pointed
exactly where you want it, and take note of where you'll

have to stand to be in the frame. Press the shutter button and run into position. A light on the camera should blink, getting faster and faster until the shutter releases. Of course, this doesn't allow you to see the image you are capturing until after you shoot it, so it may take a number of shots before you get an image you like. Just as when shooting a portrait of someone else, you will want to position your camera at an interesting angle. Try setting up your tripod at different heights, or play around with running or jumping into the frame as the shutter clicks in order to capture less static pictures of yourself.

If your camera has a rotating LCD screen, try flipping the screen so you can view it when you're facing the lens. If your LCD screen is fixed, you can position your camera in front of a mirror so you can see the reflection of the LCD screen and frame a more straightforward head-and-shoulders self-portrait. The only downside to the mirror technique is lack of spontaneity. Your self-portrait might look too posed and unnatural—remember the class picture problem?

Another simple self-portrait technique is putting the camera in front of you on Self-Timer mode, looking away from the lens until just a few seconds before the camera is about to fire, and then turning to face the camera just in time for the click. The resulting images are usually more unpredictable, as if someone else shot them for you.

If you are aiming for less traditional self-portraits, such as just showing your arm, part of your face, or your feet in the frame, one of my favorite tricks is to hold the camera by its strap at arm's length, start the self-timer, then dangle the camera back and forth or up and down with every click and just see what turns up on the screen. After all, if you don't like the results, you can always delete the shots and try something else.

Self-Portrait, Sean Dalin (sean dalin), age 19, British Columbia, Canada
Use the Continuous Shooting mode on your camera to capture a succession of shots of yourself, and then display multiple frames together as a series.
Canon EOS 20D, 18–55mm lens, tripod, ISO 200, 1/10 sec. on shutter priority, no flash
PHOTO © SEAN DALIN

Robot Rawk, Stephen McLeod Blythe (StephenMcleod), age 19, Glasgow, Scotland
What part of your personality do you want to depict? Think about it and then put on the right accessories.
Canon EOS 5D, 50mm lens, ISO 1600, 1/100 sec. at f/1.4, no flash
PHOTO © STEPHEN MCLEOD BLYTHE

How to Be a Teenager—See Below, Imogen Cunliffe (*Imogen), age 15, Lincolnshire, UK
A self-portrait can be set up. Place your camera on a tripod, trigger the shutter with a remote,
and have fun experimenting with different props, lighting scenarios, and poses.
Canon EOS Digital Rebel XTi (400D), 18–55mm lens, tripod with remote shutter release, ISO 400, 1/5 sec. at f/3.5, no flash
PHOTO © IMOGEN CUNLIFFE

If Only I Really Could, Hanah An (i am a mermaid princess.), age 17, New South Wales, Australia

A self-portrait doesn't have to show all of you—just the part you want others to see. The photographer took this creative shot by setting her camera up on a tripod, and then jumping as she released the shutter with her remote.

Nikon D80, 18–135mm lens, tripod and remote shutter release, ISO 400, 1/320 sec. at f/2.8, no flash

PHOTO © HANAH AN

Looking Up, Nicholas Gore (Nicolas Gore), age 16, North Carolina, USA

As with any portrait, experiment by shooting from different and unexpected angles.

Nikon D200, 18–70mm lens, ISO 400, 1/60 sec. at f/4, on-camera flash

PHOTO © NICHOLAS GORE

It's Only Natural
Nature and Landscape Photography

3

When I think of nature and landscape photography, I imagine ocean sunsets, a lone tree in a desert, or a blossoming flower garden. But these are only a few scenes from among endless possibilities. This chapter will help you photograph environments that range from manmade bustling urban cityscapes, to the natural wildlife of the African plain, and everything in between. The world is an amazing place. Go out and capture it!

Reflection, Júlía Runólfsdóttir, (júlía), age 14, Reykjavik, Iceland
Olympus Mju 725SW Stylus (µ725SW), ISO 80, 1/500 sec. at f/6.3, no flash
PHOTO © JÚLÍA RUNÓLFSDÓTTIR

The Great Outdoors
Landscape Basics

Defendiendo, Paula Herrero Sancho (miniqu_e), age 17, Spain
As you compose your shot, use elements, like this cannon, to direct
the viewer's eye deeper into the frame; it makes your image appear
more three-dimensional.
Nikon Coolpix L3, ISO 50, 1/410 sec. at f/6.4, no flash
PHOTO © PAULA HERRERO SANCHO

PRO TIP
If you must shoot at noon, when the light is at
its brightest and not conducive to taking
pictures, find a spot that cuts the overhead light,
like under a tree, umbrella, doorway, or bridge.
THAYER ALLYSON GOWDY

Whether you're among mountains, waterfalls, or
skyscrapers, the one thing to remember is that you are
shooting in a three-dimensional setting—one full of colors,
contrasts, and texture—and attempting to re-create it in a
two-dimensional image. The key to the 3D-to-2D
conversion is to create the illusion of depth in your
photograph.

To give depth to a landscape image, you need to use a
very narrow aperture on your camera, which increases the
depth of field of your shot. This means that more of your
frame will be in focus, resulting in overall sharpness from
front to back (or near to far). As discussed in the Getting
Started section, many cameras have a setting called

Aperture Priority mode. This mode allows you to adjust your aperture setting, and the camera will automatically select the correct shutter speed. An aperture of anything between f/10 and f/22 should be fine for most landscapes. At these f stops, the depth of field will be incredibly great, keeping nearly everything in focus.

If you have a point-and-shoot, or a camera that does not allow this, there are other ways to create depth, mostly related to how you compose your shot. The rule of thirds (see page 20) comes in especially handy when shooting a landscape, because by adding points of focus in the foreground, middle ground, and background (or bottom, middle, and top third of your frame), you're drawing the viewer's eye into the image and adding depth.

The second crucial technique for a traditional landscape image is using a wide angle. This allows you to include more in the frame, revealing more of the scene to the viewer. If you have a landscape or panoramic setting on your camera, this is an ideal time to experiment with it. Some point-and-shoot cameras even have the ability to shoot two or three frames, which you can then stitch together in-camera to generate an even more expansive view of the scene you are attempting to capture.

I like to practice shooting landscapes while on vacation. Not only is there plenty of time to experiment, but it also helps me better appreciate my surroundings and come away with mementos of my trip.

If you are drawn to more nontraditional images, try less obvious compositions, such as using a portrait orientation for a landscape shot. These types of images can be more challenging to make but can work really well for certain scenes.

It's Autumn!, Paul Lambert Vaarkamp (P.L. Vaarkamp), age 18, Vlaardingen, the Netherlands
Inherent parallel lines in a scene, such as this path in a forest in Vlaardingen, the Netherlands, can also be used to create depth in an image.
Fujifilm FinePix S6000fd (S6500fd), ISO 100, 1/420 sec. at f/5.6, no flash
PHOTO © PAUL LAMBERT VAARKAMP

It's Only Natural ✳ 63

Burn a Hole, Sean Dalin (sean dalin), age 19, British Columbia, Canada
When you expose for the background light in a backlit landscape, you can create silhouettes, which is a great way to capture interesting forms and shapes.
Canon EOS 20D, 18–55mm lens, ISO 100, 1/2000 sec. at f/5.6, no flash
PHOTO © SEAN DALIN

A Scottish Sunset, Elisabeth Scheving (Eden Photography), age 19, Minnesota, USA
When composing a landscape, look for any lines that naturally occur in your scene and use them to draw the viewer's eye into your image, such as in this silhouette of a fence in Scotland.
Canon EOS 30D, 18–55mm lens, ISO 160, 1/2500 sec. at f/4.5, no flash
PHOTO © EDEN PHOTOGRAPHY

Purakanui Bay Portrait, Chris Stevens (chris17nz), age 17, Dunedin, New Zealand
While most people will naturally use the landscape orientation to photograph a landscape, the portrait orientation can be just as effective, such as in this shot of Purakanui, Dunedin, New Zealand.
Canon EOS Digital Rebel XTi (400D), 18-55mm lens, tripod
PHOTO © CHRIS STEVENS

Mirror Perfect (Trees), Joshua Lucas (Mr Cheesecake), age 17, Essex, UK
Compose your frame thoughtfully, and put elements in the foreground, middle, and background
to create an illusion of depth, as in this landscape of Derwent Water, Lake District, England.
Pentax MZ-50 (film)
PHOTO © JOSHUA LUCAS

City Scenes
Urban Landscapes

***Sun on the Wharf**, Charlie Styr (CharlieStyr), age 17, England, UK*
Reducing an image to shades of gray, as in this black-and-white image of Canray Wharf in London, can result in a more graphically pleasing landscape.
Fujifilm FinePix S7000, ISO 200, 1/1000 sec. at f/8, no flash
PHOTO © CHARLIE STYR

PRO TIP
At the end of your shot, take a moment, then pull back for one last frame. It opens your perspective and can save you if you need to recrop.
JULIEN CAPMEIL

One thing I like about photographing cities is that they are filled with contrast—new shiny skyscrapers next to old, crumbling churches; concrete sidewalks and leafy trees; yellow taxis against a bright blue sky.

Of course, cities also present their own set of difficulties: narrow spaces; obstructed views; crowded, busy streets; and a sea of reflective surfaces, like glass windows and steel buildings. Any of these can make it nearly impossible to accurately capture the scene you want within a single frame. As mentioned earlier, a wide-angle lens is extremely useful for this, as in all, landscapes. However, it is not impossible to get good pictures without one. All it takes is some planning and patience.

Manhattan, David Nachtigall (Peacekeeper90), age 17, Schoeneck, Germany
Use slow shutter speeds to blur moving cars and people on a city street and convey the quick-moving energy of a city.
Canon EOS Digital Rebel XT (350D), 10–22mm lens, ISO 100, 1/15 sec. at f/22, no flash
PHOTO © DAVID NACHTIGALL

If you are already familiar with the area you want to shoot, pick the most opportune time to set up your shot. For example, if you want to capture the grandeur of a national landmark like the Eiffel Tower, avoid the crowds of tourists that will most likely be there at midday or on a weekend. Instead, plan to shoot your subject at night or when the landmark is closed, so you don't have to worry about people constantly walking into your picture—then you can concentrate on more important things, like the angle you would like to use.

If you always find yourself shooting from ground level, try another perspective. You have a lot of buildings to choose from—and I'm sure you can climb to the top of some of them. Shooting from above allows you to capture the sprawling size of the city and the different heights of the buildings below.

Another fun experiment is trying to capture the movement and bustle of city life. You will need a camera that will allow you to control the aperture—an SLR or high-end compact camera—as well as a tripod. Set up the tripod on the sidewalk facing an interesting building on the other side of the street. Make sure the actual street can be seen in the foreground of your frame. On your camera, use Aperture Priority mode (A or Av on most cameras) to select the narrowest aperture you can (the biggest number), which will give you the slowest shutter speed or longest exposure possible. By setting up the shot in this way, you will be able to capture the bustling business of the street, while keeping the ever-still buildings in the background.

I also like photographing cities in black and white. There is always so much going on in a city—sometimes too much. By taking away the many colors of storefront signs, peoples' clothing, and cars on the street, you remove a lot of distractions, allowing the scene to seem more moody and artistic.

Water Towers, Duluth, MN, **Adam Eckert (A. Eckert), age 20, Wisconsin, USA**
If the colors in an urban landscape aren't that compelling, shoot in black-and-white to give the image a more fine-art feel.
Canon EOS Digital Rebel XTi (400D), 28–135mm lens, ISO 100, 1/500 sec. at f/8, no flash
PHOTO © ADAM ECKERT

Street at Sunset, **Alan Chao (acd111), age 18, New York, USA**
An urban landscape becomes more interesting when taken from a unique perspective, like this diagonal frame of restaurant signs in Queens, New York.
Apple iPhone
PHOTO © ALAN CHAO

Pulling In, **Daniel Wang (chinesecommie), age 16, Florida, USA**
For a moment at dusk, the sky turns cobalt blue. By photographing an urban landscape at this opportune time, you're able to capture the city lights as well as the background detail you wouldn't be able to see in complete darkness.
Canon EOS Digital Rebel XTi (400D), 70–200mm lens, no flash
PHOTO © DANIEL WANG

Untitled, Ben Shapiro (shap43), age 19, New York City, USA

Always keep your eye out for interesting patterns, such as the perfectly aligned windows and balconies of these apartment buildings.

Canon EOS 20D, 75–300mm lens, no flash

By the Light of the Moon
Night Landscapes

A Typical Night in Front of the Opera House, Hanah An
(i am a mermaid princess.), age 17, New South Wales, Australia
Use a tripod when photographing landscapes with a slow shutter
speed to avoid camera shake and ensure that the still elements in
your photograph appear sharp.
Nikon D80, 18–135mm lens, ISO 320, 5 sec. at f/14, no flash
PHOTO © HANAH AN

PRO TIP
Try painting with light at dusk or at night. While
using a long exposure of 15 seconds to one minute, use
a strong flashlight and move it around a subject, such
as a person or building. Try not to keep the light in
one spot for too long, or you will get a big hot spot.
MATTHEW WAKEM

With all landscapes—but urban landscapes in particular—
night brings a vastly different look and feel to your
images. City lights add an almost painterly element.
It's also only at night that you are able to capture the
movement of cars with headlight and taillight trails,
or the swaying of trees as a green blur.

The key to a successful night landscape, and night
photography in general, is using a long exposure. This
means that the shutter is open for an extended period of
time, allowing more light into the camera and enabling it
to capture more detail. If you have an SLR, ensure that
your camera can take long exposures by going to Shutter
Priority mode. As discussed in Getting Started, this

setting allows you to choose the shutter speed while the camera automatically sets the most appropriate aperture for you in order to ensure a good exposure. This setting is normally signified by a Tv or S. Once you've found it, select slow speeds—20 seconds or more—using the selector dial. An SLR can typically take photos with shutter speeds as slow as 30 or 60 seconds. Many compact cameras can do similar work by using the "night" setting on your camera menu. (A manual comes in handy if you can't find the setting!)

Traditionally found only on SLRs, many cameras now also have a setting called "bulb." The bulb setting allows you to hold the shutter open for as long as you press the shutter release button, allowing you to manually control your shutter speed. To find out whether your camera has this setting, set it to manual mode and adjust the shutter speed to the slowest possible amount of time. You may eventually see the word bulb or the letter B. By setting the shutter speed to bulb, you can then hold the shutter open for as long as you want, for a much longer exposure than your camera would typically allow. To get an idea of the effect this has, imagine a 30-second exposure of the night sky, which would yield glowing starlights. Then compare it to a three-minute exposure, which would capture actual star trails, as the earth slowly rotates on its axis.

Regardless of which type of camera you use, the main problem with shooting at slow shutter speeds is camera shake, resulting in shots that look out of focus. To keep your camera still, you will definitely need a tripod, or at least a very steady, stable surface to rest your camera on for the duration of the shot.

From My Window, Frida Gruffman (~josse*~), age 19, Skelleften, Sweden
Photograph a night landscape from above to give the viewer a different vantage point.
Canon PowerShot S2IS, no flash
PHOTO © FRIDA GRUFFMAN

Last Impressions of Earth, Adam Eckert (A. Eckert), age 20, Wisconsin, USA
Looking out from the shores of Lake Superior and capturing the lights from a distance in the blue hour before night give this landscape a painterly feel.
Canon EOS Digital Rebel XTi (400D), 28–135mm lens, tripod, ISO 100, 2.5 seconds at f/16, no flash
PHOTO © ADAM ECKERT

For advanced SLR cameras, an optional add-on is a cable release, which is basically a shutter button that you can lock down for very long shutter times, such as ten minutes or more. These cables also help prevent camera shake caused when the shutter button is pressed, but are not generally available for compact cameras.

A word of warning: Before starting a very long exposure, make sure your composition is exactly the way you want it. It's really annoying when you start a five-minute exposure only to realize at the end that the horizon is crooked, or that there is a sign just on the edge of the frame you never noticed and don't want in your shot. A quick way to check composition is to take a picture of the exact scene you want to capture on regular auto mode, so you can see how it will look.

MacArthur Causeway Bridge, Kristopher Saad (usapatriot), age 16, Florida, USA
By including reflections in the bottom two-thirds of the frame, the photographer was able to create a colorful, dynamic image of this bridge in downtown Miami.
Fujifilm S9100, Sunpak 6060 tripod (Camera settings: Exposure mode: Manual, Metering:
Fujifilm FinePix S9000 (S9500), tripod, ISO 100, 5 sec. at f/4, no flash
PHOTO © KRISTOPHER SAAD

Blackpool Fireworks, **Laimonas Stasiulis (Laimonas-Stasiulis), age 20, England, UK**

Select the lowest ISO possible to reduce noise in your landscape. This, combined with a long exposure of five seconds, allowed the photographer to capture the fireworks along with the ambient light coming from the tower and illuminations on the street. The long exposure also created a sense of movement in the sea, capturing the reflection of fireworks from above.

Canon EOS Digital Rebel XTi (400D), 18–55mm lens, ISO 100, 5 sec. at f/9, no flash

PHOTO © LAIMONAS STASIULIS

Boats at Dusk, **Mateo Llosa (mateollosa), age 13, Lima, Peru**

Landscapes are usually best when they're vast, so use a wide-angle lens to capture more of the scenic elements in a shot.

Nikon D80, 18–135mm lens, ISO 100, 4 sec. at f/5.6, no flash

PHOTO © MATEO LLOSA

Into the Wild
Photographing Animals

Mull Crossing, Georgina Eltenton (georgina14), age 18, Portugal
To freeze the action of a bird in flight, experiment with fast
shutter speeds and a wider aperture.
Sony Cyber-shot DSC-N2, ISO 160, 1/400 sec. at f/8, no flash
PHOTO © GEORGINA ELTENTON

PRO TIP
Use a tripod. It may be a bit unwieldy,
but it is critical for sharp shots, and is also
necessary for long exposures.
ART WOLFE

When you're out in the field, about to frame your wildlife
picture, choosing the most attention-grabbing
composition takes patience and timing. Your subject won't
be inclined to take posing suggestions from you, so you
will have to study the animal's mannerisms—learn to
predict how it will move, when it will move, and
guesstimate just how long you have to press the shutter.
Because it may take a while for you to get the shot you
want, it helps to set up your camera on a tripod so you
won't have to hold it steady while waiting for that magic
moment.

When composing your photograph, keep in mind that
viewers tend to be drawn to wildlife shots where the

animal seems to be eerily staring back at them. Try to shoot from the subject's eye level and wait for it to look directly into the lens before you click.

You'll often be unable to get close to your subject, so it's useful to have a long lens. If you have a digital SLR camera, a lens of 100mm and longer should be fine, particularly one that can zoom to 300mm. Then manually zoom in on the subject's eyes (or any other part) by turning one of two rings on the lens, usually the larger one, to adjust the zoom. Much like the focusing ring (which is usually the smaller of the two rings), the zoom ring will physically shift the lens to provide greater magnification.

If you have a compact point-and-shoot, you will normally see a magnification number—something like 3× or 6× or 12×. For wildlife photography, anything from 6× and above should be fine. You normally operate the zoom function on a point-and-shoot camera using two buttons. One is most likely marked by an icon of many trees, signifying a wide angle; the other is marked with only one tree, signifying a close-up shot. For distance shooting, use the button with the single tree to zoom in on your subject.

Note that some compact cameras also have a digital zoom that enables you to zero in even more on your subject. As discussed on page 13, it is best to avoid using this feature because it can result in a severe loss of detail and contrast. The last thing you want in a nature shot is a loss of detail, as you are trying to capture as many natural colors, textures, contrasts, and other elements as possible for a realistic-looking photo.

A camera's "continuous shooting" function is especially useful for photographing an animal in motion. This function allows you to press down on your shutter to take a succession of images in quick sequence. To find it, look for a button with an icon that shows a series of rectangles on top of one another, symbolizing multiple photos in a pile. If you don't see this on your camera, go to your menu options, select "Shooting mode," and then select "Continuous."

Remember that photographing an animal in motion also requires fast shutter speeds to freeze the action. Keep your shutter speeds high by raising your ISO to around 200 to 400, or use a wider aperture, such as those between f/2.8 and f/5.6. With a point-and-shoot camera, check your manual to see whether your camera has a designated sports or action function, which will instruct the camera to automatically use high ISO speeds, wide apertures, and/or continuous shooting.

Leopard, **Peter Woodside (Peter W), age 18, County Louth, Ireland**
A wildlife shot is more compelling when the subject seems to be staring at the viewer, as in this portrait of a leopard in Nairobi Safari Park, Kenya. Canon EOS Digital Rebel XTi (400D), 50–500mm lens, ISO 1600, 1/200 sec. at f/6.3, no flash
PHOTO © PETER WOODSIDE

Simba, Peter Woodside (Peter W), age 18, County Louth, Ireland
A zoom lens will help you capture more dangerous wildlife from a safe distance, like this young lion photographed while on a safari in Masai Mara, Kenya.
Canon EOS Digital Rebel XTi (400D), 50–500mm lens, ISO 200, 1/640 sec. at *f*/9, no flash

African White-backed Vulture, Peter Woodside (Peter W), age 18, County Louth, Ireland
Photographing animals takes timing and patience. For example, you need to wait for an animal like this African white-backed vulture to fly into your frame before pressing the shutter.
Canon EOS Digital Rebel XTi (400D), 50–500mm lens, ISO 200, 1/500 sec. at *f*/8, no flash

Goshaw, Peter Woodside (Peter W), age 18, County Louth, Ireland
Much as in portraits of people, you can use a wide aperture (small *f*-stop number) to get a shallow depth of field in order to isolate the animal from the background.
Canon EOS Digital Rebel XTi (400D), 50–500mm lens, ISO 200, 1/500 sec. at *f*/8, no flash

Sheep on a Hill, Joshua Rozad (jbr_jbr), age 15, Ontario, Canada
Remember to sometimes step back from the animals and frame them in their natural surroundings to convey a sense of their environment.
Nikon D40x, 55–200mm lens, ISO 400, 1/160 sec. at f/5.6, no flash
PHOTO © JOSHUA ROZAD

Life Magnified
A Macro World

Veins, Frida Gruffman (~josse*~), age 19, Skelleften, Sweden
Plants are great subjects on which to practice macro photography because of their innate intricate colors and patterns.
Canon PowerShot S2IS, 1/320 sec. at f/4, no flash
PHOTO © FRIDA GRUFFMAN

Macro photography is the art of taking pictures that are so close up, they reveal microscopic details that cannot be seen with the naked eye or even with the aid of a zoom lens.

Plants and insects are common macro subjects, but things like pebbles on a beach, a sheet of handmade paper, a paint-chipped door—really, anything—can become an interesting image when magnified. You will see subtle details, ranges of color, textural nuances, and intricate shapes that you otherwise would not be able to make out.

To uncover these details, you need to enable the macro mode on your camera. Nearly every camera has a macro mode. On a point-and-shoot system, the macro

PRO TIP
When the weather turns on you, think small. Even in the worst conditions, you can shoot a macro. Foggy days are also rich in color, and long exposures can enhance those hues.
ART WOLFE

Monarch Butterfly, Tad Arensmeier (Tad 20D), age 19, Missouri, USA

The depth of field in your image gets shallower the closer you get to your subject, which is something to keep in mind in macro photography. Note that everything behind this monarch butterfly is blurred.

Canon EOS 20D, 70mm lens, ISO 400, 1/250 sec. at f/7.1, Canon Speedlite 550EX flash

PHOTO © TAD ARENSMEIER

function has its own button; just look for the flower symbol—generally, a small tulip. Press the button to enable the function, and your camera will be able to focus in on subjects much more closely than in normal mode.

Of course, the fact that macro mode magnifies subjects so significantly can also work against you. If you're photographing a plant, for example, check for bugs, bits of dirt, or dead leaves before shooting. One of my pet peeves is taking what I think is a great macro shot, only to find out later on that I captured imperfections unintentionally. While you may be able to fix some of these later in programs like Photoshop (page 125), getting rid of them at the scene will save you from a time-intensive retouching process.

From a technical standpoint, one challenge of macro photography is adjusting the depth of field, or how much of the image is in focus. Since your depth of field always decreases as you focus closer and closer in on your subject, too shallow a depth of field in macro shots means that only a small part of the image will be in focus. If you were to shoot, say, a chopped log, only a small band of the wood would be in focus, and the rest of the log would be out focus. To solve this, you can "stop-down," which means selecting narrower apertures (larger f-stop numbers), such as f/8 or f/12. As you stop-down, more of your subject will be in focus, not just a narrow strip, enabling you to capture more detail in the final photograph.

If your camera doesn't have a built-in macro mode (possible, but highly unlikely), check out your local photo store for macro lenses that you can attach to your camera.

Desde Abajo (From Below), Itsaso Arizkuren Astrain (Absent Minded), age 15, Iruña, Spain
Turn your lens on subject matter you think would look interesting super close up.
Sony Cyber-shot DSC–W55, ISO 200, 1/60 sec. at f/2.8, no flash
PHOTO © ITSASO ARIZKUREN ASTRAIN

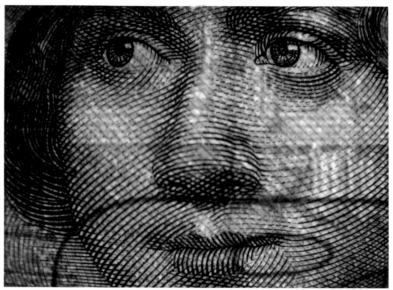

Swedish 50kr Bill, Frida Gruffman (~josse*~), age 19, Skelleften, Sweden
Macro photography allows you to see the details and patterns in everyday things you otherwise wouldn't see.
Canon PowerShot S2IS, 1/13 sec. at f/2.7, no flash
PHOTO © FRIDA GRUFFMAN

Macro Bugs, Liam Higginson (HiggySTFC), age 15, Shropshire, England, UK
Check the subject for dirt or anything else that you don't want a magnified view of. A speck of dirt magnified could have ruined this shot.
Nikon D40, 18–55mm lens, ISO 200, 1/400 sec. at f/8, no flash
PHOTO © LIAM HIGGINSON

Cecropia Caterpillar, Joshua Rozad (jbr_jbr), 15, Ontario, Canada
Use the macro setting on a point-and-shoot camera to magnify
the details found in small subjects.
Canon PowerShot S3IS, ISO 80, 1/250 sec. at f/2.7, black backdrop, no flash
PHOTO © JOSHUA ROZAD

The Bright Side
Capturing the Colors of Nature

Water Lilies, **Frida Gruffman (~josse*~), age 19, Skelleften, Sweden**
Choose a time of day when the light is not too harsh so that the
sun doesn't wash out the colors in your picture.
Canon PowerShot S2IS, 1/640 sec. at f/4, no flash
PHOTO © FRIDA GRUFFMAN

A very important aspect of nature photography is color.
Unless you are aiming for a specific effect, such as
extreme colors or black and white, you will want the color
in your photographs to look natural and realistic.

The season and time of day of your shoot will affect
the color tones in your image. If you are shooting under a
clear, sunny sky, the bright sunlight will likely saturate
the colors in your image; if you are shooting on an
overcast day, dispersed light will create a more flat light,
evening out colors and resulting in more natural-looking
scenes.

Glaring sun can be a problem, especially during
summer months, when days are longer and light is

PRO TIP

Envision the exact image you want, and then go
out and work and work and work until that
vision is realized through your camera.

PAUL NICKLEN

brighter. It's helpful to keep in mind the "magic hour." The magic hour is a term you'll hear a lot of photographers refer to as the one hour in the early morning after the sun rises above the horizon, or the one hour just before the sun sinks below the horizon line at dusk. At these times, the sun creates long shadows that add interest and texture to nature shots. The light is also warmer, giving your images richer, more natural color.

Be on the lookout for this one-hour window. Once the sun comes over the horizon in the morning, it rises rapidly and you can easily miss the best light. A high sun will cause the shadows in your scene to appear shorter, resulting in less contrast. If you wait too long in the afternoon, on the other hand, you risk getting too close to sunset, again missing optimum lighting conditions.

Fall and spring offer lots of color, and winter can cast a beautiful white blanket over a landscape, offering its own attractive photo opportunities. Keep in mind,

however, that snow reflects light and tricks your camera into underexposing a shot. This is because the industry settings of your camera's meter will always expose for a medium gray; think of it as the camera's default meter reading. So, let's say it is a bright, sunny day and you want the snow in your picture to appear its natural white—you will need to compensate for this by overexposing your shot by one to two stops.

If you're using a point-and-shoot camera, you can do this by putting the camera on manual mode, and increasing your exposure compensation setting by +1 or +2. (If you do not know how to find your exposure compensation setting, refer to the instruction manual, as menu settings differ from camera to camera.) If you are using a more advanced digital SLR camera, also put the camera on manual mode, then increase the exposure by using a longer shutter speed or wider aperture. (If this sounds confusing, go back to page 16 and reread Basic Tech Terms to refresh your memory.)

Regardless of season, ensuring that your camera is in the correct white-balance mode is another technique to get the color you're looking for. "White balance" is a term used to describe the way digital cameras color-correct their images. Different light sources emit different colored light, and various lighting conditions will affect the color in your images in different ways. Look at the three examples shown here.

White Balance 1, 2, and 3, Charlie Styr (CharlieStyr), age 17, England, UK
This series of photos of white lilies illustrates the difference white-balance settings can have on color in a photograph. Photo number one is at the correct white balance, and was taken using a setting for sunlight (and the day was in fact sunny). Photo number two is slightly wrong, and was taken with the fluorescent light setting. Photo number three is dramatically wrong, with the whole image appearing red/orange, and this was taken with the shade setting.
Canon EOS Digital Rebel XTi (400D)
PHOTO © CHARLIE STYR

Ultimately, the white-balance mode on your camera determines the warmth or coolness of an image—whether it has an orange-reddish tint or a more bluish tint. Most cameras will normally be in auto white-balance mode, which means that they will automatically calculate the white balance for any given situation. However, in many newer cameras, you can select the white balance manually, which is something to experiment with if you are not getting the results you want with the automatic setting.

To white-balance manually, find the white-balance menu, normally a button labeled WB on SLRs and more advanced cameras. On compact cameras, you may have to look at the menu to find the white-balance settings. You will normally be presented with some preset choices, for example: daylight, cloudy, shade, tungsten light (good for any scene that's lit with old-fashioned lightbulbs), and fluorescent light (the white strip lights you usually find in gymnasiums, grocery stores, and industrial buildings). These presets are examples from my camera; yours may have different options.

By choosing the most appropriate white-balance setting for the scene you are shooting, you will keep a realistic color spectrum in your images. The red flowers won't be overly red, and the sky will keep its natural blue color. It's very important to keep your colors true, or a scene will look fake or overly digitally enhanced.

Beautiful White Lane, Paul Lambert Vaarkamp (RW), age 18, Vlaardingen, the Netherlands
Snow tricks your camera into underexposing a shot, so when photographing winter landscapes, remember to compensate for this by overexposing your shot by one or two stops.
Fujifilm FinePix S6000fd (S6500fd), ISO 100, 1/420 sec. at f/4.5, no flash
PHOTO © PAUL LAMBERT VAARKAMP

Dew-Covered Fern, Chris Stevens (chris17nz), age 17, Dunedin New Zealand
If there's not a cloud in sight, then put a black backdrop behind your subject to call attention to its color.
Canon EOS Digital Rebel XTi (400D), 18–55mm lens, ISO 400, 1/100 sec. at f/5.6, no flash
PHOTO © CHRIS STEVENS

Flood, Liel Bomberg (Liel Bomberg), age 16, Tel Aviv, Israel
Vivid plants against a gray, rainy-day backdrop allow the colors to pop.
Fujifilm FinePix S5200 (S5600), ISO 400, 1/10 sec. at f/3.3, no flash
PHOTO © LIEL BOMBERG

Sun Flowers, Sean Dalin (sean dalin), age 19, British Columbia, Canada
Timing your shot just before the sun rises (or sets) will allow for a
backlit image that still renders the colors accurately.
Canon EOS 20D, 10–22mm lens, ISO 100, 1/250 sec. at f/3.5, no flash
PHOTO © SEAN DALIN

Getting Wet
Underwater Photography

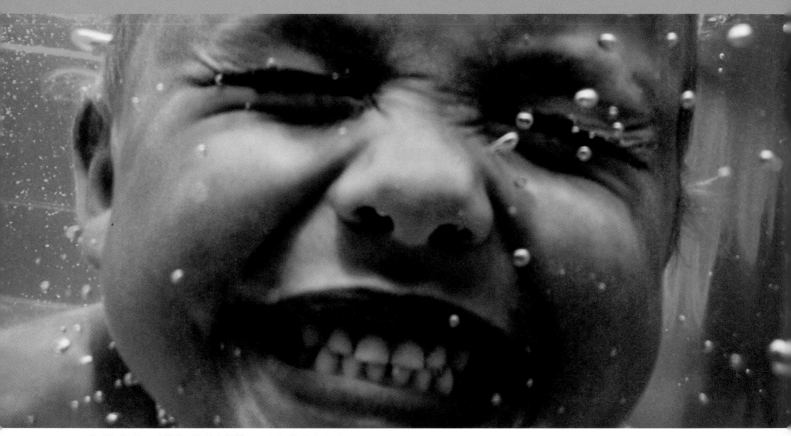

Andri in the Water, Júlía Runólfsdóttir (Djúlí), age 14, Reykjavik, Iceland
If your underwater subject is nonthreatening, then get as close as
you can for a better shot.
Olympus Mju 725SW Stylus (µ725SW), ISO 80, 1/500 sec. at f/3.5, no flash
PHOTO © JÚLÍA RUNÓLFSDÓTTIR

PRO TIP
Don't skimp on the shots, especially with
wildlife. It may take many frames to get
one good shot.
ART WOLFE

The major difference between underwater photography
and regular photography is what comes between your
subject and your lens. Air is relatively clear, but water
contains many particles, and because of the way it refracts
light, your images will appear soft, often without much
contrast. When you are shooting underwater, stay close to
your subject to minimize this loss of quality. A little
patience is also a good thing, as most fish are happy to
come close to you.

Most cameras are not designed to go underwater, so
you will need to buy either a separate disposable camera
that can, or underwater housing for your camera at your
local camera shop. Underwater housing can cost

anywhere from $200 to $2,000 depending on the quality of the housing and the type of camera you need it for. Many stores also sell specially designed, watertight plastic bags that zip up to keep your camera dry. While this is a much cheaper option and is great for swimming pools or shallow water, I don't recommend it for prolonged underwater use or shooting at greater depths. Water is dense, and the deeper you get, the more pressure it puts on your camera, making the camera more susceptible to damage.

Particles in the water become more visible when a flash is used, so it is much better if you have a separate flash—called a "strobe"—that is not attached to your camera. The strobe (which will also need underwater housing, called flash housing) will still illuminate the particles, but if you angle it properly at the side of your camera, the reflected light will bounce off the particles at an angle instead of hitting them straight on and fully illuminating them. In this way, the particles won't be as visible in the final image. An underwater strobe is usually attached to your camera with a cable, so you can hold it wherever you want. Getting closer to your subject will also reduce the number of distracting particles in your shot, and will increase the contrast and sharpness of the image. If you're shooting marine life, the flash of light may startle or disturb them, so be cautious as you approach your subjects.

You may not need a strobe if you are shooting in shallow water. Natural light penetrates water for only about thirty feet. The deeper you go, the more the light starts to drop off, significantly decreasing your visibility. If you are planning to photograph marine animals on a diving excursion in deeper waters, it might be interesting to frame a shot of the animal from below, to get the dramatic effect of light shining through the water's surface.

It goes without saying that safety is always a concern when shooting underwater. In addition to the proper photographic equipment, you need the proper swimming, snorkeling, or diving gear, depending on the situation.

Not a good swimmer? You can photograph underwater creatures without getting wet if they are in an aquarium. Photographing fish (or other wildlife) through glass poses a unique set of challenges. Glass is a reflective surface, so if you're using an in-camera flash or strobe for your shot, you will most likely capture glare in your final image instead of the fish. The best way to avoid this is to use existing light. Most aquariums are lit from above or from inside to illuminate the details—bright colors, intricate scales, tentacles—of the creatures housed in them. By turning off your flash and increasing your ISO to its max, you will increase the digital sensor's sensitivity to that light and be able to capture those details. Keep in mind, we did mention in the Film Speed section on page 18 that increasing your ISO increases your chance of noise appearing in a shot, so you'll have to experiment with the ISO levels on your own camera to see how far you can go without sacrificing too much image quality.

Dancing Coral, Liel Bomberg (Liel Bomberg), age 16, Tel Aviv, Israel
Incorporate techniques you've learned from other essays into your underwater pictures, such as showing only part of your subject for a more eye-catching composition.
Fujifilm FinePix S5200 (S5600), ISO 200, 1/75 sec. at f/3.2, no flash
PHOTO © LIEL BOMBERG

Another option in a situation like this is to widen your aperture (use a smaller *f*-stop number) to allow more light to hit your digital sensor, resulting in the same effect. The drawback to this option is that your image won't be as sharp and will have a shallow depth of field. So if there are multiple creatures in the aquarium, most likely only the one in the foreground will be in focus, and the others will appear blurred.

To add more elements to your decision-making, if the animal in the aquarium is moving, you will probably need a faster shutter speed to freeze the action. As we mentioned in the Exposure section on page 18, it will take some finagling to figure out the perfect balance of aperture, film speed, and shutter speed for the particular shot you want to take. You should also shoot using multiple combinations so you can compare the differences and know better the next time you're in that situation which settings worked best. Of course, there's always the option of turning off the flash and putting the camera on automatic so that it makes the decisions for you, but where's the fun in that?

Lion Fish, Nicole Kubin (nck1925), age 17, Connecticut, USA
If you must take an aquarium shot with the camera's built-in flash, then make sure you're close enough to the glass to avoid unwanted glare.
Canon PowerShot SD600 (IXUS 60), 1/8 sec. at *f*/2.8, on-camera flash
PHOTO © NICOLE KUBIN

Jellyfish in Space, Kirsty Marr (seventy-five), age 17, Texas, USA
Because of the low light in the aquarium, the photographer used Shutter Priority mode. It resulted in a dark background, with the jellyfish glowing bright against it as if they were spaceships.
Olympus C-7070 Wide Zoom, ISO 80, 1/30 sec. at *f*/2.8, no flash
PHOTO © KIRSTY MARR

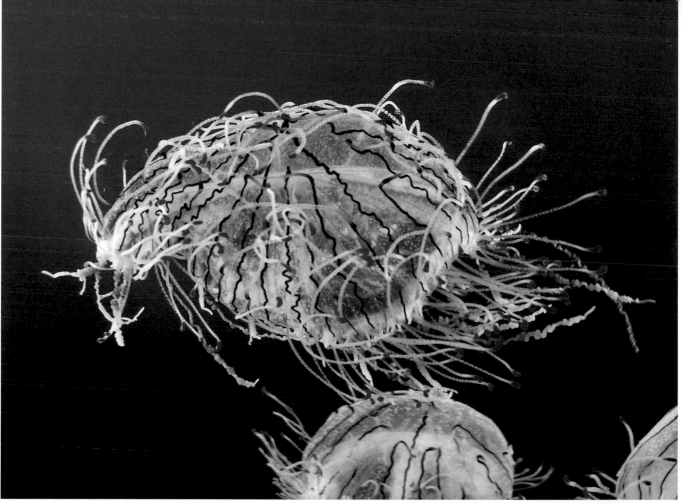

Candy Strips, **Kristy Marr (seventy-five), age 17, Texas, USA**
There's often enough light in aquariums to shoot your subject without a flash. This photographer used a macro setting to reveal the small, pink details in the jellyfish.
Olympus C-7070 Wide Zoom, ISO 80, 1/15 sec. at f/2.8, no flash
PHOTO © KIRSTY MARR

Fun at Water Polo Practice, **Sarah Lee (Sarah Lee), age 17, Hawaii, USA**
You can use natural light if you are shooting in shallow waters, like a swimming pool. This picture was taken at sunrise.
Canon EOS Digital Rebel XT (350D), 50mm lens, ISO 100, 1/500 sec. at f/5.6, no flash
PHOTO © SARAH LEE

In the Moment:
Sports and Action Photography

Speed is always exciting. But actually capturing fast-moving action is perhaps one of the most difficult photographic techniques to get right. This chapter covers three common strategies used to photograph subjects in motion—freezing motion, motion blur, and panning. Follow along, and soon you'll be snapping your shutter in tune with your subject, no matter how fast it's traveling.

Against the Force of Gravity, **Sarah Lee (Sarah Lee), age 17, Hawaii, USA**
Canon EOS Digital Rebel XT (350D), 70–300mm lens, ISO 200, 1/500 sec. at f/8, no flash
PHOTO © SARAH LEE

Freeze Frame
Capturing Peak Action

Peak Performance, Sarah Lee (Sarah Lee), age 17, Hawaii, USA
Use an interesting point of view to help convey the action of the sport you are photographing.
Canon EOS Digital Rebel XT (350D), 18–55mm lens, ISO 400, 1/640 sec. at f/16, no flash
PHOTO © SARAH LEE

PRO TIP

Sometimes the best way to capture a decisive moment is to slow down. Most people want to rush or "pounce" on a picture, but the reality is that there are many decisive moments. Take time to think about your photograph—how you want to compose it and what it is that you're looking to capture—and the photograph will come more easily.

VINCENT LAFORET

When taking photographs of sporting or action events, timing—knowing when to press the shutter—is everything. It is crucial to become familiar with the sport you want to shoot. Whether it's ski jumping, football, or motor racing, getting to know the sport's pace and rhythm will allow you to anticipate the best times to snap a photo.

One thing to keep in mind, especially if you're shooting with a lower-end digital camera, is shutter lag. Shutter lag is the time elapsed between pressing the shutter release button and when the camera actually takes the picture. On many SLRs, this isn't a huge issue because the shutter lag is usually only about 0.1 seconds—not long enough to make a difference in your final image.

Snap, Benjamin Ang Zhen Ming (nccair), age 18, Singapore, Singapore
Using the Continuous Shooting mode on a point-and-shoot would have helped this photographer capture multiple frames in succession—before, during, and after the peak moment.
Canon PowerShot S6IS, ISO 200, 1/1600 sec. at f/4.5, no flash
PHOTO © BENJAMIN ANG ZHEN MING

However, with more compact cameras, the lag may be long enough for the camera to actually miss the split-second you wanted to capture.

The best way to solve the shutter lag dilemma is to spend time getting used to the way your camera works. Experiment and get used to how fast it takes your camera to focus, and how long it takes between focusing and actually taking the shot. This will help you anticipate when to press the shutter.

For really fast-paced action shots, sometimes focusing on the subject once just isn't enough to capture that peak moment. That's when "continuous autofocus" comes in handy. The Continuous Autofocus function is available on nearly all SLR cameras and on some non-SLRs. It is extremely useful in sports photography because it allows you to follow your subject with the camera and have the subject always be in focus (instead of having constantly to refocus) until you are ready to take your shot. This means you can concentrate on what's happening in the frame rather than on technical aspects, which is really important in a fast-paced photography situation.

To find the Continuous Autofocus function, look for a button labeled AF. If your camera has a drop-down menu, you should be able to select Continuous Autofocus, sometimes known as servo AF or constant focusing.

Another useful function for action photography is "continuous shooting." This function allows you to capture a series of shots in succession with one press of the shutter. Think of continuous shooting as a safeguard function—it ensures that you capture the precise moment you wanted, not a split-second before or after. For example, one of my favorite sports is soccer, and when I think of photographing it, I know that capturing a player in midair with the tip of his toe on the ball would make a very powerful image. With continuous shooting, I can press the shutter once as the player is about to jump and raise his leg, telling the camera to fire a series of shots

and know that one of them will capture the image I want.

To find the Continuous Shooting mode on an SLR, look for "Shooting mode," often a button with three or more squares piled on top of one another. If you are using a compact camera, simply search for "Shooting mode" in the drop-down menu.

Combining the Continuous Autofocus and Continuous Shooting modes opens a whole new range of possibilities. Using the same soccer game as an example, you can now follow a soccer player in your viewfinder with the shutter half pressed (thus keeping him in focus); when you see him getting ready for a big kick, you can press down the shutter completely, and your camera will shoot a burst of images. The speed at which the series of shots are fired varies from camera to camera, but generally you will get two or three photos per second.

Skiing Under a Sunrise, Joshua Beam (Josh Beam), age 15, Texas, USA

In a backlit shot like this, it is more beneficial to expose for the sun (versus the subject) because it automatically gives you the fast shutter speed you need in order to stop the action.

Pentax K110D, 18–55mm lens, ISO 200, 1/2000 sec. at f/13, no flash

Sweep the Leg, Sean Dalin (sean dalin), age 19, British Columbia, Canada

Pump up the drama by manipulating your picture as the photographer did in this shot by increasing the contrast and saturation and sharpening the image.

Canon EOS 20D, ISO 100, 1/250 sec. at f/3.5, Canon Speedlite 430EX flash

Said the Sun to Shine, Sarah Lee (Sarah Lee), age 17, Hawaii, USA

When taking an action shot, it helps to prefocus so you are ready to shoot when your subjects reach the exact position you want to capture.

Canon EOS Digital Rebel XTi (400D), 50mm lens, ISO 200, 1/1250 sec. at f/10, no flash

PHOTO © SARAH LEE

One After Another
Shooting a Sequence

Dad Surfing Set Black Borders, Chris Stevens (chris17nz), age 17,
Dunedin, New Zealand
A zoom lens was crucial to capturing from a distance local
surfing legend (and the photographer's father) Peter Stevens
getting nailed by a big wave.
Canon EOS Digital Rebel XTi (400D), 70–300mm lens
PHOTO © CHRIS STEVENS

✳
PRO TIP
Take your camera away from your eye and point
it in the direction of the action. This enables you
to get high and low camera angles quickly,
and accidents are one of the greatest
joys of photography.
JIM ERICKSON

In much the same way as you can use continuous
autofocus and continuous shooting to capture a peak
action shot, you can also use these functions to capture a
whole string of events. Using my favorite soccer example,
if you wanted to shoot a sequence revolving around a
particular player scoring a goal, you could capture the
moment his toe hits the ball, another image of the ball
flying through the air, and then the same ball pounding
into the net.

The key to shooting an effective sequence of images
is first thinking about when you want your sequence to
begin, and exactly when you want it to end. As in the
soccer example, the ideal sequence should tell a story and
be in chronological order. For example, if you want to
shoot a sequence of a slower paced sport, like golf, the
following shots would probably be vital: the golfer

Sal Flip, Sean Dalin (sean dalin), age 19, British Columbia, Canada
The Continuous Shooting mode allows you to trigger the shutter in rapid succession in order to capture each frame of the action as it's unfolding.
Canon EOS 20D, 10–22mm lens, ISO 100, 1/200 sec. on Shutter Priority, no flash
PHOTO © SEAN DALIN

walking up to the tee, the golfer taking a swing, the ball flying through the air, and the ball landing on the green.

Once you have decided which images you want for your sequence, you simply frame and take each shot as you would any picture, making sure your subject is in focus throughout the sequence. After you have finished, you can instantly review the pictures with your digital camera; if there are any images that don't meet with your approval, delete them right away, using only the best for your final sequence.

One great way to display a sequence of images is to line them up side-by-side in chronological order, showing the story line. Doing this always reminds me of a flip-book—the kind of book that animates the movement of a subject as you flip through the images.

Into the Mediterranean, Sarah Lee (Sarah Lee), age 17, Hawaii, USA

If you look closely, you can see that this shot consists of only two friends taking the plunge together into the Mediterranean Sea. This effect can be achieved by having your camera on a tripod, and using Continuous Shooting mode to capture people as they run past the camera. Then in Adobe Photoshop you sequence multiple images together to create one image that shows progression.

Canon EOS Digital Rebel XT (350D), 18–55mm lens, ISO 200, 1/320 sec. at f/11, no flash

Motion Blur
Panning

Fisico, **Adam Eckert (A. Eckert), age 20, Wisconsin, USA**
A monopod helped this photographer keep the camera steady as he
practiced panning while focusing on this race car circling the track.
Canon EOS Digital Rebel XTi (400D), 100–300mm lens, monopod, ISO 100, 1/200 sec.
at f/10
PHOTO © ADAM ECKERT

Panning is a powerful photographic technique, especially
in sports and action photography. In the movies,
"panning" is observed when a filmmaker moves across a
scene with his or her camera, tracking a moving object. In
photography, panning is used to create a sense of speed in
an otherwise still image. When panning is done correctly,
the main subject appears sharp against a blurred
background, giving the illusion of movement. Panning is
most effective when the subject is moving along a
horizontal plane—such as a car traveling from the left side
of your frame to the right. If there is any vertical
movement, such as a runner raising or lowering his legs, it
will not appear as sharp.

PRO TIP
While panning is used mostly to capture fast
action shots, it is also a great way to make a
chaotic background look more artistic by
creating a beautiful blur of color and shapes,
which in turn will isolate your subject. Play
around with different shutter speeds and
aperture settings to experiment with the effect.
MATTHEW WAKEM

As you probably know by now, a fast shutter speed usually results in a crisp image. However, when you are panning, you need to use a slower shutter speed to achieve the blurred background. I recommend shutter speeds of 1/30 sec. or 1/40 sec. The panning effect at these shutter speeds will differ from subject to subject, so it's best to experiment on your own with different speeds.

To select your shutter speed on an SLR or similar camera, find the Shutter Priority mode, often signified by an S or a Tv. Once you are in this mode, choose the shutter speed with your select dial, often near the shutter release, and then the speed you want. On point-and-shoot cameras, there is normally no way to manually control shutter speeds, and you cannot get the slowest desired speeds, but you can still use the camera's automatic speed setting to achieve some motion blur.

As an example, let's say you want to use the panning technique with a moving car. With your camera in hand, look at the car through the viewfinder and follow it with your lens, keeping it in the center of the frame. It helps to keep your feet flat on the floor and turn only the top half of your body while doing this, so that the camera stays steady. Press the shutter and continue to track the car with your camera. If you've done it correctly, the car should be sharp in your final image, in the center of the frame, while the background appears streaky and blurred.

If you are shooting your subject from a distance, you will want to use a shutter speed that is on the faster end of the slow scale, like 1/40 to 1/60 sec. This is because the distance will require you to zoom in on your subject, exaggerating the blur of the camera. When you are closer up, and shooting from a wider angle, the situation is the opposite, so you may want to choose a shutter speed on the slower end, from 1/20 to about 1/30 sec.

Panning is open to a lot of experimentation. Try zoom panning, which only really applies to SLRs that can zoom in while taking photographs. To perform a zoom pan, you simply take a photograph at a manageable shutter speed, say 1/40 sec., and zoom in on the subject as you are taking the photo. This effect shows a blurry movement toward the center of the image, and can be a dramatic technique to isolate a subject.

Skate, Max Preissner (m.preissner), age 15, Ann Arbor, Michigan, USA
Feeling ambitious? Try following yourself in motion, as did this photographer who captured himself on his skateboard.
Nikon D80, 18–135mm lens, ISO 125, 1/160 sec. at f/8, no flash
PHOTO © MAX PREISSNER

Track Cyclists, Chris Hepburn (Chris Hepburn), age 18, Stafford, UK
In this photograph of two speed cyclists, a flash was used to cause the racers to stand out more from the blurred racetrack.
Nikon D200, 27–70mm lens, ISO 800, 1/800 sec. at f/2.8, Nikon SB-600 AF Speedlight flash
PHOTO © CHRIS HEPBURN

Marching Band, Karlos Harbor (bharbos), age 17, Missouri, USA
Panning can be used for situations other than fast action, as in this image,
where the technique was used to isolate the subject and create an artistic blur.
Canon EOS Digital Rebel XTi (400D)

Radical 31, Jake Yorath
(jake yorath photography),
age 18, England, UK

A steady hand is
necessary to execute a
successful panning
shot, especially when
the subject, like this
race car, is moving at
top speed.

Nikon D50, 00–200mm lens,
1/30 sec. at *f*/22

PHOTO © JAKE YORATH

*Model Train Moving
Fast*, Dale Rothenberg
(Pianisimo), age 16,
Connecticut, USA

When panning is
applied correctly,
your main subject
appears sharp
against a blurred
background, giving
the illusion of
movement.

Nikon D50, 50mm lens,
ISO 800, 1/25 sec.
at *f*/1.8

PHOTO © DALE ROTHENBERG

Telling It Like It Is
Photojournalism and Documentary Photography

5

Perhaps one of the greatest things about being a photographer is having the ability to tell a story through pictures. By capturing candid moments in time, photographers are able to record history, promote awareness about a certain place or event, and most important, motivate change. Photographers who make these real-life images their livelihood are called photojournalists or documentary photographers. There are stories worth telling everywhere—at home, in foreign countries, even underwater—and this chapter will show you how to capture them.

The Concerned Photographer
Telling a Story Through Pictures

Survivors, Mateo Llosa (mateollosa), age 13, Lima, Peru
An important element to any story is the people involved, such as
this photograph of two elders who survived the earthquake in Peru.
Nikon D80, 18–135mm lens, ISO 320, 1/125 sec. at f/5.6, no flash
PHOTO © MATEO LLOSA

A successful shot can give viewers a real feeling for what
was going on when the image was captured. Some good
examples of pictures that tell stories are the images you
see in newspapers and news magazines like *TIME* and
Newsweek. While pictures like these are used primarily to
illustrate a written story, often the reader is compelled to
look at the words only because of the immediate impact of
the images.

Imagine the rush of emotion a photograph of a
natural disaster like Hurricane Katrina, which hit New
Orleans in 2005, can cause in viewers. By photographing
an aerial shot of the overall flood damage, battered
buildings, a crowd of people crying, or a combination of

PRO TIP
Always be a nice person to the subjects and
communities you cover. Don't scorch the earth for the
next photographer who will surely come after you.

DAVID MCLAIN

all three, you get a real sense of how devastating this
event was for a lot of people. Capturing newsworthy
images like these is referred to as photojournalism.

Photojournalists are often considered the silent heroes
of the photo world, risking their lives on a daily basis to
bring a wide range of topics to our attention—war coverage
from Iraq, photo essays of famine in Africa, or even
stories that hit closer to home, like gang life in East L.A.

Of course, your story doesn't have to be as hard-hitting
as those mentioned above. There are photojournalists, like
the late Cornell Capa (brother of famed war photographer
Robert Capa mentioned in the Pro Tip), who considered
themselves photographers of humanity. A photographer
for *LIFE* magazine, Cornell Capa followed the campaign
trail of former presidents like John F. Kennedy and turned
his lens on a diverse range of subjects that included
ballerinas, Ford Motor Company engineers, and Russian
Orthodox monks.

Having died in 2008, he is widely remembered for
coining the term "the concerned photographer," which is a
phrase that resonates with teens like me today. For me,
being a concerned photographer means caring enough
about the world around you to pay attention to people,
places, and events worth capturing. It also means sharing
those captured moments with others, so that they too
might take notice.

If there is a situation or person in your life that you
feel passionate about, whether it's homelessness in your
local neighborhood or a student at your school whom you
believe deserves some recognition, then hone your
photojournalistic skills by taking the time to tell that
story—and capture each frame with care.

Be Happy, Peter Woodside (Peter W), age 18, County Louth, Ireland
Candid shots of local people can give the viewer a sense of far-off
places, like this shot of friendly kids in the village of Kambui, Kenya.
Canon EOS Digital Rebel XTi (400D), 18–55mm lens, ISO 400, 1/100 sec. at f/7.1, no flash
PHOTO © PETER WOODSIDE

Burn It to the Ground, Sean Dalin (sean dalin), age 19, British
Columbia, Canada
Tell the story of an important event by photographing the
scene as the action unfolds.
Canon EOS 20D, 18–55mm lens, ISO 100, 1/60 sec. at f/9, on-camera flash
PHOTO © SEAN DALIN

Faith to Go On, Mateo Llosa (mateollosa), age 13, Lima, Peru
Your story doesn't always need to be told with a hard-hitting
photo. For example, here the photographer hints at the strong
relationship many older people in his country have with
religion by showing an elder in a humble setting with a
Virgin Mary calendar in the background.
Nikon D80, 18–135mm lens, ISO 160, 1/25 sec. at f/4, no flash
PHOTO © MATEO LLOSA

Hero, Mateo Llosa (mateollosa), age 13, Lima, Peru

In order for your story to grab a viewer's attention, it's crucial to capture real-life emotion. The child in this photo has just survived an earthquake in Peru and walked for miles along the highway to beg for donations from passersby.

Nikon D80, 18–135mm lens, ISO 320, 1/1000 sec. at f/5.6, no flash

PHOTO © MATEO LLOSA

Quaking Ruin, Mateo Llosa (mateollosa), age 13, Lima, Peru

You can use photographs to promote awareness of natural disasters, and hopefully inspire viewers to act.

Nikon D80, 18–135mm lens, ISO 250, 1/250 sec. at f/3.5, no flash

PHOTO © MATEO LLOSA

Bored in Class, Mateo Llosa (mateollosa), age 13, Lima, Peru

Photojournalism or documentary images are not set up beforehand; they depict life as it unfolds, as evidenced by the candid photograph of these kids at school in the Peruvian jungle.

Sony Cyber-shot DSC-H5, ISO 320, 1/15 sec. at f/3.5, no flash

PHOTO © MATEO LLOSA

My So-Called Life
Shooting Everyday Moments

Poor Sole, Hanah An (i am a mermaid princess.), age 17,
New South Wales, Australia
Train your eye to find beauty in simple subject matter, like
this still life of sneakers by a sun-drenched window.
Nikon D80, 18–135mm lens, ISO 320, no flash
PHOTO © HANAH AN

PRO TIP
Think about what you're interested in.
Make a list, then pick one thing,
and take some pictures of it. Keep taking
pictures of the same subject for
one month and see what happens.

MAXINE BEURET

Shooting your everyday life is an excellent way to practice
storytelling through pictures. Because our daily lives can
seem monotonous—school, home, hanging out with friends—
it isn't always easy to feel inspired to take pictures of day-
to-day reality. But if you take time to look at what's going on
around you, you'll find a wide range of photo opportunities.

One great way to get into the groove of finding picture-
worthy subjects is to look at your local newspaper or
school bulletin for interesting events you can attend,
camera in hand, of course. Basketball games, school plays,
concerts—it doesn't matter. The challenge lies in finding
unique frames wherever you are, so make it a point to go to
at least one event a week and just keep shooting.

Mischa, Katharina, and Joseph, Dale Rothenberg (Pianisimo), age 16, Connecticut, USA
Find out what's going on in your local community or school, and actively seek out photo opportunities. For example, a high school play as shown in this photo.
Nikon D80, 55–200mm lens, ISO 1000, 1/40 sec. at f/5.3
PHOTO © DALE ROTHENBERG

Recently, I was asked to photograph a youth festival in Shrewsbury, a quaint town in England not too far from where I live. I had never really attended this festival before and was surprised to find that it featured live music, sports, martial arts demonstrations, and other fun things. Had I not been asked by an acquaintance to shoot this event, I probably would have spent the day in front of a computer. Instead, I left the youth festival with some great images, some of which would even be used for promotional material for the event for the following year.

However, if you find that you are more fascinated by people than actual events, then try a different storytelling approach. Ask a friend or relative if you can follow them around for a week or two and document their lives. When you're actually looking for pictures, more often than not you will find them—whether it's a candid shot of your sister sleeping or even a still life of her worn-out sneakers strewn casually on the floor. Together, these snapshots tell the story of who she is better than a single portrait ever could: the way she laughs (or not), her sense of style, and how she spends her leisure time.

Of course if you can't find a willing subject, you can take on a more creative, long-term project and snap a picture out the same window at the same angle at the same time every day for a full year. As you look at how the images progress, what story are you able to uncover? Does the same scene unfold before your eyes each day? Or are you discovering subtle changes with every shot that you never really noticed before?

Action I, Charlie Styr (CharlieStyr), age 17, England, UK
Attending local festivals and events can encourage you to take an interest in what's going on closer to home. This shot of a martial artist was taken at a summer youth festival in England.
Canon EOS Digital Rebel XTi (400D), 50mm lens
PHOTO © CHARLIE STYR

Cab Blur, Ben Shapiro (shap43), **age 19, New York, USA**
Use different techniques, such as panning, to turn everyday scenes into artistic frames. This New York City scene of a man crossing the street as a cab whizzes by does just that.
Canon EOS Digital Rebel XTi (400D), 75–300mm lens
PHOTO © BEN SHAPIRO

Lost, Liel Bomberg
(Liel Bomberg), age 16,
Tel Aviv, Israel
My friend Tal with a
wreath of flowers beside
my house in Israel.
Canon PowerShot A720IS,
ISO 80, 1/40 sec. at f/4.8,
no flash

Which, Jackson White (jaacson),
age 15, British Columbia, Canada
Bring a different viewpoint to
common occurrences, such as
this shot of football players
from within a huddle.
Sony Cyber-shot DSC-W55, ISO 100,
1/100 sec. at f/7.1, no flash

The World Around You
Travel Photography

Liceu Flea Market, Sarah Lee (Sarah Lee), age 17, Hawaii, USA
Don't limit yourself to photographing only famous sights. Travel photography should give viewers a glimpse of local haunts, like this Liceau Fleamarket in Barcelona, Spain.
Canon EOS Digital Rebel XT (350D), 18–55mm lens, ISO 100, 1/60 sec. at f/5, no flash
PHOTO © SARAH LEE

If you've ever flipped through a travel magazine or photo book, you'll notice that travel photography combines a bit of everything—portraits, landscapes, night shots, and more.

Like photojournalism, travel photography is most effective when it tells the story of your trip and chronicles your experiences. This is why it's important to take your camera with you wherever you go. Whether you're traveling abroad or just spending a weekend at a cabin a few hours from where you live, you never know when you're going to see something camera worthy. If you don't have your camera, it's a lost photo op.

PRO TIP

Good travel shots should tell a story—local food shots, portraits, the sleepy city at dawn, street signs. Liken it to writing in your journal: This is what I saw, this is what I tasted, this is what I heard, these are the people I met.

THAYER ALLYSON GOWDY

If you're traveling to a foreign place, simple snapshots of found objects can be interesting. I was recently in France with my family and friends, and one day when the weather was bad I began exploring the house we were staying in, and found some things I wouldn't have normally noticed, such as this large flowerpot in the French garden (shown to the right). What's so interesting about a flowerpot? The pot caught my eye because we would never have had a pot like this at home, and the shutters in the background were also very telling of the place's architecture and design. Details like these make for the best travel photography, where your main goal is to capture a sense of place.

To get a sense of a new environment, take time to walk around and acclimate yourself to it. One of the best places to start is a local market. A market can really give you insight into another culture. You not only get a glimpse of actual people from the area, but you become familiar with their everyday lives by examining the things being sold—such as food and crafts.

When shooting national landmarks, or important places of worship in an area, always be aware of the local customs. Be respectful of the place you're shooting and the people who live there. This is also key when approaching someone to ask whether you can take their portrait. It's crucial to get some good portraits in travel photography, but you need to have a willing subject. If you are polite and ask nicely, most people will allow you to take their picture. Some may not want you to stop! For subjects who are a little shy, try to be encouraging. It helps to talk to your subjects as you take their picture; crack a few jokes to get them to smile and feel comfortable.

Flowerpot in France, **Charlie Styr (CharlieStyr), age 17, England, UK**
Keep your eye out for environmental still life shots, such as this flower pot in the middle of a garden in Bargemon, France.
Canon EOS Digital Rebel XTi (400D), 18–55mm lens, ISO 800, 1/30 sec. at f/4.5, no flash
PHOTO © CHARLIE STYR

Glenn, Neil Dorgan (Neil Dorgan), age 18, Wicklow, Ireland
Capture candid portraits, like this one of the photographer's friends playing guitar
on a beach in Barcelona, Spain, to help tell the story of your trip.
Holga 120CFN, Fujifilm CS 120 Fujicolor Reala film (ISO 100)
PHOTO © NEIL DORGAN

Derwent Water, Peter Woodside (Peter W), age 18, County Louth, Ireland
Use wide-angle landscapes, like this shot of Derwent Lake, in Keswick, England, to convey a sense of place.
Canon EOS Digital Rebel XTi (400D), 18–55mm lens, ISO 200, 1/2000 sec. at f/4.5, no flash
PHOTO © PETER WOODSIDE

Waiting for the Flight Home, Júlía Runólfsdóttir (júlía), age 14, Reykjavik, Iceland
Travel photography should chronicle your experience, even if you're just waiting at an airport.
Olympus Mju 725SW Stylus (µ725SW), ISO 125, 4 sec. at f/3.5, no flash
PHOTO © JÚLÍA RUNÓLFSDÓTTIR

Austrian Market, Charlie Styr (CharlieStyr), age 17, England, UK
Photographing a public place from a distance, like this bird's-eye view of locals going about their daily lives, is another way to convey a sense of place.
Fujifilm FinePix S7000, ISO 160, 1/480 sec. at f/6.3, no flash
PHOTO © CHARLIE STYR

Silencio, Joshua Lucas (Mr Cheesecake), age 17, Essex, UK
Don't always go for the big picture. Travel photography also encompasses detail shots unique to the location, such as this Portuguese sign at the Olhao Nature Reserve.
Nikon Coolpix 7600, no flash
PHOTO © JOSHUA LUCAS

The World of Post-Processing

This book is designed to show you how to capture the images you want in-camera—but sometimes a photo doesn't work out the way you imagined it would. Welcome to the world of post-processing! This chapter presents numerous techniques you can apply to an image after you've taken it: Remove that unwanted zit; make your colors more vibrant; or even make an abstract mosaic from a series of photos. All you need is a computer and one (or more) of the programs discussed to enhance your photos or create something based entirely on your imagination.

To Change or Not to Change

Why Alter an Image

Crop Shots, Charlie Styr (CharlieStyr), age 17, England, UK
Cropping can make an image more effective by removing extra, unwanted space around your subject.
Canon EOS Digital Rebel XTi (400D), 18–55mm lens, no flash
PHOTO © CHARLIE STYR

BEFORE

AFTER

So you've taken your pictures—now what?

While being a good photographer means getting the composition, exposure settings, and other elements right when taking the shot, digital photography has opened up a whole new world of possibilities for improving upon your pictures after capture. There are several reasons why you would want to alter an image, but the first question that comes to my mind is, why not?

By altering an image, you can make it more lifelike or more dramatic, depending on the look you're going for. There may also be aspects of your image that you want to improve. Maybe your picture is too dark or not crisp

enough. These issues can be resolved (somewhat) with a bit of retouching—the common term for (digitally) enhancing or altering an image.

Cropping is one of the simplest ways to improve an image. It basically involves cutting off an unwanted part or parts of a picture, ultimately reshaping it. For example, you take a photograph of a city skyline, but when you get back to your computer and examine the shot, you find that there is too much sky in the frame. With a simple crop, you can take some of the sky out and are left with a more panoramic image of a skyline. (For more on cropping, see page 126.)

BEFORE

AFTER

Or what if you took a macro photograph of flowers but later found the colors were somewhat drained, or not as vibrant as they appeared in real life? This is where **image adjustment** tools come in handy. They allow you to adjust things like brightness, contrast, saturation, and tint/hue.

Still other times, you may discover that your image is soft or blurred, in which case a **sharpening** tool can be used to make the picture crisper and clearer. Do be careful about sharpening an image too much. Too much sharpening can lead to digital artifacts appearing; remember learning about noise on page 18? It also can make the subject appear too detached from the background, which will make your image look unrealistic and unappealing.

Saturation Shots, Charlie Styr (CharlieStyr), age 17, England, UK
Use the saturation tool in moderation to improve the overall color of the final image.
Canon EOS Digital Rebel XTi (400D), 50mm lens, no flash
PHOTO © CHARLIE STYR

Sharpen Shots, Charlie Styr (CharlieStyr), age 17, England, UK
A little sharpening can make an image look naturally crisp.
Canon EOS Digital Rebel XTi (400D), 50mm lens, no flash
PHOTO © CHARLIE STYR

BEFORE

AFTER

Many photo-editing programs, like Photoshop, have tools that allow you to erase parts of an image, such as a speck of dust or a small bug on that perfectly crisp leaf. Like all the retouching options, these tools, when used in moderation, are helpful for creating a more perfect yet realistic image, especially when there is no opportunity for a reshoot.

Of course, postproduction doesn't always involve taking something away from an image. You can add to an image, too. The **vignette** tool adds a darkish border to the corners of an image, creating a moodier, more dramatic look. **Blur** is another effect you can add. When used correctly, it can impart an ethereal, romantic look to an image, as well as show motion.

It is possible to overretouch an image, such as when you oversaturate your colors to the point where the image is just a swamp of bright reds, greens, and blues. Or when you sharpen an image so much that each speck of dust stands out. It's best to retouch an image just enough so that it still looks realistic. If you've done a good job, viewers shouldn't notice that the image has been altered at all.

Clone Shots, Charlie Styr (CharlieStyr), age 17, England, UK
Make this fruit shot look more appealing by removing the dark spot from the banana.
Fujifilm FinePix S7000
PHOTO © CHARLIE STYR

Don't Follow the Crowd, Peter Woodside (Peter W), age 18, County Louth, Ireland
Retouching doesn't always mean erasing something. In this image of starlings in flight, the one bird was simply turned around using Photoshop—he wasn't really flying the opposite way.
Canon EOS Digital Rebel XTi (400D), 50–500mm lens, ISO 400, 1/4000 sec. at f/6.3, no flash
PHOTO © PETER WOODSIDE

Jump!, Liel Bomberg (Liel Bomberg), age 16, Tel Aviv, Israel
Combine two perfect poses to create the perfect image, such as this
cool shot that was actually made from an image of a girl jumping and
a self-portrait of the photographer.
Fujifilm FinePix S5200 (S5600), ISO 64, 1/420 sec. at f/5.6, no flash
PHOTO © LIEL BOMBERG

Just Believe, Joshua Rozad (jbr_jbr), age 15, Ontario, Canada
Create the impossible! This paper crane looks like it's floating over some-
one's hand, but the photographer erased the model's other hand, which was
holding the crane, using Photoshop.
Canon PowerShot S3IS, tripod, ISO 400, 1/15 sec. at f/2.7, black backdrop, no flash
The photographer used Photoshop Elements 5.0, I decreased saturation, increased contrast,
color-burned the background, sharpened this photo, and erased the extra hand.
PHOTO © JOSHUA ROZAD

Dive Lapse, Sarah Lee (Sarah Lee), age 17, Hawaii, USA
Stitch multiple frames together to show a sequence, such as these images
of a boy diving that were shot using Continuous Shooting mode and later
combined into one frame using Photoshop.
Canon EOS Digital Rebel XT (350D), 18–55mm lens, ISO 800, 1/500 sec. at f/16, no flash
The photographer used Adobe CS3's Camera Raw to adjust color tones, add vignetting, and
adjust exposure.
PHOTO © SARAH LEE

The World of Post-Processing ✳ 123

Techie Tools

Morning Joy, Sarah Lee (Sarah Lee), age 17, Hawaii, USA
This senior portrait was taken in the early morning. After capture, the
photographer used Adobe CS3's Camera Raw to adjust color tones,
sharpness, and exposure.
Canon EOS Digital Rebel XTi, ISO 100, 1/1000 sec. at f/1.8, no flash
PHOTO © SARAH LEE

There are hundreds of imaging programs out there, some
of which are free. Here are a few of the more popular
programs that you can use to create a library of your
photos or for simple retouching (as described on pages
120 to 122).

Picasa from Google (http://picasa.google.com) is an
excellent, free after-capture software that enables you to
both organize your images and do basic editing. If you
are using a Mac, the iPhoto software built into your
machine is similar to Picasa, but with even more detailed
adjustment capabilities.

Picasa automatically searches your computer for
photographs when you first install it, and then builds up
the library by folders. Picasa also allows you to
automatically adjust brightness, contrast, and colors
using an auto-adjust mode, which can be useful if you
need a quick fix. You can manually adjust shadows,
highlights, and overall brightness too, which gives you
more creative control. Standard effects include the ability
to convert colored photos to black and white or sepia. To
find these editing options, double click on a photograph

Curling, Joshua Rozad (jbr_jbr), age 15, Ontario, Canada
The photographer used Photoshop Elements 5.0 to increase contrast and
sharpen this photo of smoke coming off a cone of incense at night.
Canon Powershot S3IS, Aperture Priority, 1/250 sec at f/2.7, on camera flash
PHOTO © JOSHUA ROZAD

when you are in your library and Picasa will bring up the editing options.

For more serious editing, try out Gimp, another free software, available at www.gimp.org. Gimp has many of the features—including filters, masking tools, and a cloning tool to remove unwanted dust, for example—found in more advanced software like Adobe Photoshop, placing it a step above programs like Picasa and iPhoto. It's a good stepping-stone to Photoshop, because you can use Gimp to find out if you actually need the additional features found in more high-end programs like Photoshop before spending money on them. Once you've installed Gimp, its help files are very useful for working out the features of the program.

Adobe Photoshop is probably one of the most famous image-editing programs available for Windows and Macintosh. There are numerous versions available for download—from the Elements version, which contains the more basic aspects of the program, all the way to Adobe CS3, widely used by professional photographers worldwide. This version has more advanced features not found in the Elements version, including the ability to combine multiple exposures and a vanishing-point tool. Unless you plan to do a lot of retouching, you may be able to spare yourself the additional expense. Visit www.adobe.com for more information on the different versions.

When considering which software is right for you, keep in mind that many schools that offer photo classes or have a photo department have copies of Photoshop (and other programs) for students to use, an option that might save you money.

No matter what image-editing software you choose, nearly all photographs can do with a little enhancing. The following "cheat sheet" of technical tips is somewhat based on Photoshop (I am using Adobe Photoshop CS2). However, the tips and instructions can also be adapted to similar programs, like Gimp, and other versions of Photoshop.

Sharpening

To sharpen an image, start by going to
Filters ► Sharpen ► Unsharp Mask.

Don't be confused by the term **Unsharp Mask**; it is a sharpening tool. Play around with the sliders until you get the look you want. This will also help you get comfortable with what the sliders actually do. As a guide, **amount** is the degree of sharpening; **radius** is the distance around each pixel to be sharpened; and **threshold** is how much change should occur to be acceptable.

Increase the **amount** to make the image very sharp, then move the slider down until the image looks pleasing to the eye, ideally, as it would look in real life. You can also play with **radius** and **threshold** for other effects.

Window Light, Jamie Ringoen (jamie.marie), age 16, Colorado, USA
This photographer gave her image an artistic look by using Photoshop to desaturate the colors, increase the contrast to create a beautiful backlit glow, and add two textures.
Canon EOS 60D, 50mm lens, ISO 400, 1/200 sec. at f/1.4, no flash
PHOTO © JAMIE RINGOEN

Cropping

As explained on page 120, cropping is a basic way to enhance an image. In Photoshop, crop an image by selecting the rectangular marquee tool, which looks like a square in the toolbar. Use the tool as a frame to select whatever part of the image you want to keep. You can also add specific dimensions above the image in the toolbar, such as 4 × 6" if you are printing to paper of that size. Once you've framed the image with the selection tool:

Go to **Image ➤ Crop.**

This crops the image, leaving only the parts you have selected. If you don't like the results:

Select **Undo** by going to **Edit ➤ Undo**, and try again.

Adjusting Contrast

Levels are an interesting aspect of Photoshop (and Gimp), and can be used to increase contrast and enhance the bright or dark areas of an image.

Go to **Image ➤ Adjustments ➤ Levels** to open up a Levels window.

When the window is open, you will see a histogram (see Photography Speak p.141) of the bright areas in the image, and you can drag the sliders below the graph. The left slider adjusts the blacks, the middle slider adjusts midtones, and the right slider adjusts whites. When you drag the sliders, you will see the colors of the image change. Keep playing with the levels until the colors appear as you want them to.
    If you don't want to manually adjust each color level, there is another option:

Go to **Image ➤ Adjustments ➤ Auto-Levels.**

This tells Photoshop to automatically adjust contrasts to how it thinks they should be. Generally this works well, but if you don't like the result or are looking for a specific effect, I suggest using the fully manual controls.

Another fun effect is converting colored images to black and white. This effect often works well for city shots. You can also apply a sepia effect, which uses brown tones and works wonderfully with portraits, giving the picture a historical feel. To apply a black-and-white effect:

Go to **Image** ➤ **Adjustments** ➤ **Black and White**.

This will automatically convert the image to black and white.

To make it sepia, first convert the image to black and white, then:

Go to **Image** ➤ **Adjustments** ➤ **Variations**.

You will see a display of colors. Add one red and one yellow, and your image will be converted to sepia.

Adjusting Color Saturation
If you want to increase or decrease the intensity of the colors in your photos, you can play around with adjusting the saturation.

Go to **Image** ➤ **Adjustments** ➤ **Hue/Saturation**.

You will see the saturation slider, and this can be adjusted left and right for increased color saturation.

Rub-a-dub-dub, Elisabeth Scheving (Eden Photography), age 19, Minnesota, USA
Color saturation was used to make the colors pop in this portrait of a baby sitting in a red bucket outside a chicken coop.
Canon EOS 30D, 85mm lens, ISO 160, 1/1250 sec. at f/2, no flash
PHOTO © ELISABETH SCHEVING

A Leap Into Fall, Elisabeth Scheving (Eden Photography), age 19, Minnesota, USA
With some thoughtful cropping, this photographer was able to emphasize the subject's feet jumping in a pile of leaves.
Canon EOS 30D, 85mm lens, ISO 200, 1/1600 sec. at f/2.5, no flash
PHOTO © ELISABETH SCHEVING

The Wish to Fly, Susannah Benjamin (ireland1324), age 14,
Connecticut, USA
Merge images to create a juxtaposition with a dreamlike feel,
such as this photo that combines a photo taken in Venice, Italy,
with a portrait.
Nikon D80, 18–135mm lens, no flash
PHOTO © SUSANNAH BENJAMIN

PRO TIP
Keep a visual diary. I have everything from interesting
websites, films, and books, to sketches, exhibition tickets,
and useful contacts. It's a great source for inspiration.

ALYS TOMLINSON

There are many, many more creative, fun things you can do with your pictures after you've taken them, beyond the color adjustments and other effects mentioned previously.

Lomo

One idea is trying a "Lomo" effect. Lomo photographs are taken with cheap, plastic toy cameras called Lomos (not too difficult to see the connection there). The images have a somewhat vintage feel, and the colors often look oversaturated, with lots of contrast. Lomos were made popular by artists like Andy Warhol, and while they are still available and making a comeback, you can replicate the look with some simple adjustments to "Hue and Saturation" in Photoshop or similar programs.

Collage

Perhaps you have taken a series of pictures, or are beginning to see a unifying theme in your work. One way to combine these images to make a completely new überimage is to create a collage. A collage is a very simple way of mixing images together (and you can even use other materials like magazine cutouts or found objects). For old-fashioned collages, all you need is a pair of scissors, some glue, and a sturdy board on which to mount the materials. If you are using only digital images and want to go the tech-savvy route, just use Photoshop or a similar program to create a new canvas of a reasonable resolution (I recommend 1280 × 1024 if you want to use it as wallpaper for your computer, or an even higher resolution if you want to print and display it). Once you have created your digital canvas, simply drag in a selection of photos and resize and place them as you want.

Double Exposure

Similar to collage, a double exposure or layered image allows you to combine multiple exposures into one photograph. As an experiment, set up your camera on a tripod so that it stays in the same place. Now, shoot a series of frames of the same person in different positions but using the same background. For example, it could be a person climbing a chair to change a lightbulb; if so, you would capture them in front of the chair, standing on the chair, reaching up toward the lightbulb, and squatting down to jump off the chair. Then, in Photoshop or another image-editing program, you could layer the images one on top of the other—again, the key is that the background stay exactly the same except for the person's position—making it look like you cloned your subject so they could be in several different places at the same time.

Diptychs

Another way to combine images is simply to place or hang them next to each other to create a diptych (two related photographs) or triptych (three related photographs). This is similar to the idea discussed on page 106 in terms of telling a story through images, but the story doesn't have to be as literal as it would be in a documentary-type series. Instead, you might just think the pictures go well together and evoke the same look and feel, such as combining a close-up portrait of your best friend with another close-up portrait of your best friend's pet, because, after close inspection, you suddenly realized they look a lot alike!

Really, the possibilities are endless. I hope this essay, and all the others that came before it, inspire you to try new things and to share your experiences with fellow photographers so we all can continue to learn from each other and create compelling imagery.

Friends, Danica Cheetham (Danica Jade), age 16, Queensland, Australia
If you can't pick one shot you like, use them all to create a fun mosaic of multiple frames.
Fujifilm FinePix S7000
PHOTO © DANICA CHEETHAM

Technicolor, Lucy Rodriguez (Lucee.), age 16, California, USA
You don't need paper and glues to do a digital collage. Just layer multiple elements using Photoshop, such as in this self-portrait.
Canon PowerShot SD1000, ISO 200, 1/4 sec. at f/2.8, no flash
PHOTO © LUCY RODRIGUEZ

Fall Against Me, Hanah An (i am a mermaid princess.), age 17, New South Wales, Australia
Pair related images in order to tell a visual story, such as this diptych of a girl against her window next to a shot of a sunset and rain.
Nikon D80, 18–135mm lens, no flash. Aperture Priority mode. Increased brightness/contrast, soft light filter, screen filter, altered levels, and sharpened image.
PHOTO © HANAH AN

Mosaic 2, Chris Stevens (chris17nz),
age 17, Dunedin, New Zealand
Try combining images to create
an abstract "mosaic," as this
photographer did in Photoshop.
You'd never guess the tiles in this
shot were actually images of a
Gibson Les Paul electric guitar!
Canon EOS Digital Rebel XTi (400D),
70–300mm lens, tripod
PHOTO © CHRIS STEVENS

Tiny, Roxana Hojat (foxanaburger), age 18, Pennsylvania, USA
Combining film with digital techniques can result in a
winning combination, such as in this self-portrait diptych.
These images were shot with a Polaroid film camera, then
layered and juxtaposed using Photoshop.
Polaroid Spectra 1200SI, Polaroid 990 film
PHOTO © ROXANA HOJAT

What Next?

Getting Your Pictures Seen

One of the greatest things about taking pictures is being able to share them. Photo-sharing communities on websites such as Flickr.com and Ringo.com are a popular way to get your photos seen. Another way is through social networking sites like MySpace.com and Facebook.com. Or you can build your own blog. In this chapter, we'll talk about some other ways to get your pictures seen, as well as include tips on how to profit from your images. After all, you can have fun taking pictures and make some money at the same time.

Jump for Joy, Jamie Ringoen (jamie.marie), age 16, Colorado, USA
Canon PowerShot A610, no flash
PHOTO © JAMIE RINGOEN

Photo Contests, Exhibits, and Books

Photography contests are a way to get your work seen by the right people. According to Maria Wakem, coauthor of this book and former editor of New York–based student photography magazine *PDNedu* (www.pdnedu.com), a lot of photo editors, advertising art buyers, gallery representatives, and other creative types turn to photo contests to discover up-and-coming talent. Maria adds that *PDNedu* has its own annual student photo contest, open to high school and college students worldwide, and the magazine's parent publication for professional photographers, *Photo District News (PDN)*, holds a number of annual contests that focus on a wide range of topics, from portraiture to travel photography. All *PDN* contests have a separate student category and a discounted entry fee for student participants—all you need is a student ID as proof. Organizations like the Student Photographic Society and the Society for Photographic Education (SPE) also list competitions or calls for entries and submissions on their websites: www.studentphoto.com and www.spenational.org, respectively. In addition to these resources, you should regularly check your local newspaper or school bulletin for contest listings.

Not the competitive type? Then maybe a photo exhibit is more up your alley. Most schools with photography or art programs offer various ways (and a space) for students to showcase their photographs. If your school doesn't, think about taking matters into your own hands. "Guerrilla art exhibits" are organized and promoted by students themselves, usually in nontraditional spaces like dorm basements, neighborhood cafés, or even a school gymnasium after hours. The

Spring 2008 Flood, Joshua Rozad (jbr_jbr), age 15, Ontario, Canada
Josh submitted this image to his local newspaper and it was subsequently published as a "Photo of the Day" on April 28, 2008.
Nikon D40x, 55–200mm lens, tripod, ISO 200, 1/250 sec. at f/5.6, no flash
PHOTO © JOSHUA ROZAD

exhibits run for one or two days and can be a great way for young artists to get feedback on their work, get noticed by potential clients, or even make a sale.

If you have a lot of images you want to show but don't have the resources to organize an all-out photo exhibit, another fun option is to make a photo book. Websites like Shutterfly.com, Lulu.com, Blurb.com, and (for Mac users) the bookmaking options on iPhoto are all inexpensive, creative ways to put a bunch of your images together as a gift for friends and family members, to sell on your website, or to keep as a memento of your work for you to look at for inspiration.

Are you passionate enough about photography to consider it as a career? Many of the professional photographers who shared tips in this book started out by working for their school newspaper. Most school papers don't pay for pictures, but the practice and lessons you learn can be invaluable down the road. An added bonus: Getting published in the paper gives you work samples and credibility to start your own photo business while still in school.

Selling Your Images

The opportunities for making money from your photographs are limited only by your creativity, time, and energy. Why not, for example, start a local portrait business, taking senior portraits of classmates, shooting local bands in your school for their MySpace page, photographing people's pets, or covering events like birthday parties or bar mitzvahs? Start by word-of-mouth networking or put up a MySpace, Flickr, or other type of page specifically for your photography "business," which you can use to show potential customers examples of your work.

Decide in advance what your rates will be, and be sure to factor in not only time but also expenses such as transportation and food. Discuss in advance how the final photographs will be delivered—will you give them a CD of JPEGs, or will you supply them with prints if they want them? If so, who will pay for the prints? Will you give them all the images you shoot as is, or will you spend time editing out the bad ones, sharpening them, adjusting cropping, and so on? Any extra work you put in should be factored into your fee. It is also always smart to put everything in writing to make sure you and your "client" are on the same page, even (or especially!) if it's a friend or family member. This way, you can avoid awkward misunderstandings later by getting clear on the terms up front.

Small local businesses in your community are another possible customer base. A lot of small businesses need photographs but can't afford the cost of commercial photography. Put together a portfolio of work samples and stop by some local stores to see if they could use your services. If they seem interested, agree on a reasonable rate, and it's a win-win situation. They get the images they need at a price they can afford; you get more work samples and a reference for a future job.

Untitled, Elisabeth Scheving (Eden Photography), age 19, Minnesota, USA
Elisabeth was both the maid of honor and the photographer for her brother's wedding! She would set up each shot and then run into the frame while someone else pushed the button. Having these in her portfolio has helped her get hired for other weddings as well.
Canon EOS 30D, 85mm lens, ISO 100, 1/200 sec. at f/5.6, no flash
PHOTO © EDEN PHOTOGRAPHY

COPYRIGHT 101

Copyright is the ownership of intellectual property, such as a photograph or literary work, within the limits prescribed by a particular country's (or international) law. In the United States, as soon as you create a unique photograph, you legally own the exclusive right to print, distribute, and copy that photograph throughout your lifetime, plus seventy years. Anyone who wants to use that photograph in any of those ways within that period of time must obtain permission from you (or your benefactors) before doing so. To make a copyright more official, you can register your work with the U.S. Copyright Office (www.copyright.gov). This is advisable if you are going into the business of photography because it makes it a lot easier for you to take legal action should anyone violate your copyright. Of course, the same copyright protection laws apply to work others create, so be careful of copying or distributing other photographers' work or you could find yourself in a lot of trouble! For more information on copyright, visit Photo District News' website:

http://www.pdnonline.com/pdn/resources/is-it-legal/index.jsp

Shetland Sheep, Joshua Rozad (jbr_jbr), age 15, Ontario, Canada
Josh shot this image as part of a paid photo shoot for a local sheep farm and wool business. The business owner, an acquaintance of Josh's family, asked him to photograph her sheep herd and property after seeing his work on Flickr.
Nikon D40x, 55–200mm lens, ISO 400, 1/125 sec. at f/5.6, no flash
PHOTO © JOSHUA ROZAD

Engage, Sean Dalin (sean dalin), age 19, British Columbia, Canada
The couple in this photo hired Sean to photograph their engagement and wedding. They'd heard of him through word of mouth and checked his photos out online.
Canon EOS 20D, 10–22mm lens, ISO 400, 1/160 sec. at f/3.625, no flash
PHOTO © SEAN DALIN

Wishes on Red Paint, Jamie Ringoen (jamie.marie), age 16, Colorado, USA
Jamie's image of dandelion seeds on red paint was published in *Teen Ink* magazine.
Canon PowerShot A610, 1/80 sec. at f/2.8, no flash
PHOTO © JAMIE RINGOEN

Golden Droplet, Joshua Rozad (jbr_jbr), age 15, Ontario, Canada
Josh's image of a water droplet was spotted on Flickr by the owner of a vegetable oil trading business, who is now paying Josh a small fee to use the image on his business website.
Canon PowerShot S31S, tripod, ISO 80, 1/250 sec. at f/2.7, on-camera flash
PHOTO © JOSHUA ROZAD

Your Stock Options

Another way to make money from your images is through stock photography, specifically microstock. Have you ever seen a picture in a newspaper or magazine with Getty or Corbis listed in the photo credit? These are two examples of traditional stock agencies.

Stock agencies are huge online photo libraries of images shot mostly by professional photographers from all over the world. Magazines, newspapers, advertising agencies—just about anyone looking for a photo—can access these libraries and purchase the use of an image. The price of the image generally depends on how the image will be used, where it will run, and how long it will be used, and can range from $100 to $100,000. When an image is purchased, the photographer and the stock agency each get a percentage of the sale. (These percentages are agreed upon in advance.)

Not just anyone can sell images through stock agencies. You have to apply, and even if you are accepted, each image has to go through a rigorous review process before you are able to sell it online. As we were writing this book, Getty Images, one of the largest stock agencies in the world, entered into a partnership with Flickr. The details of the partnership have yet to be determined, but it could mean business opportunities for some of the members of the Teenage Photographers group. Overall, the chances of a teen photographer getting into a big stock agency are slim, but there are less daunting options.

A "microstock" agency is like the baby brother (or sister) of a big stock house. It works like a traditional stock agency in that your images have to be accepted before you can sell them on the site, but because the images sell for lower rates—anywhere from one to ten dollars—these agencies are usually more willing to accept images from younger, less established photographers. Microstock sites are cropping up all over the world. Some, like CanStockPhoto.com based out of Halifax, Nova Scotia, were even started by students.

Before taking the plunge into the stock photo world, take some time to read about the stock industry and microstock. A few good sites to check out are www.pdnedu.com, www.stockartistsalliance.org (you can download their free magazine Keywords to learn industry lingo and definitions), www.istockphoto.com (the first microstock site ever created), and www.microstockdiaries.com (a blog for people who sell photos in the microstock market).

Whether this book inspires you to start a full-fledged photography business or just to shoot more (and better) pictures, we hope that, in some way, we've helped you stay creative!

PERMISSIONS AND RELEASES: A NECESSARY REQUIREMENT

Securing permissions is something you will most likely need to think about if your photos will be used in advertising or promotions, especially if they include recognizable faces or places. Most stock photo agencies will require you to submit a model release or property release, depending on the nature of the photograph. These releases are basically written agreements signed by the person in the photograph, or property owner of the property in the photograph, that permit you to use the photos in question commercially (i.e., for advertising, promotion, or profit). The rules for when a release is required by law may differ from country to country. Generally, in the United States, you do not need a release to publish or display images of people taken in a public place, as long as those pictures will not be used to sell a product or service. For more information on releases and to see some sample documents, a great resource is the American Society of Media Photographers' website: www.asmp.org. Just plug the words "model release" into the search box and you'll find a list of related reading material.

Meet the Pros

William Abranowicz is a contributing photographer to *Condé Nast Traveler*. His work appears regularly in *The New York Times Magazine, Town and Country*, and *Elle Décor*. His advertising campaigns include Banana Republic, Ralph Lauren, Tommy Hilfiger, and Target, and his work is included in public, corporate, and private collections worldwide, including the National Collection of the Smithsonian Museum in Washington, D.C., The Getty Museum in Los Angeles, Bibliothèque Nationale in Paris, the International Center of Photography in New York, and the Thessaloniki Museum of Photography in Greece.
www.williamabranowicz.com
PHOTO © XANDER ABRANOWICZ, 2003

Maxine Beuret is a photographic artist who explores different cultural environments in the context of time passing, in particular, looking at fading aspects of life and human activity. She received an MA in Photography from De Montfort University in Leicester, UK, in 2007. That same year, she was selected as one of *PDN's* 30 New and Emerging Photographers to Watch. Her work has been included in numerous exhibitions, including the Lennox Contemporary Gallery in Toronto (*Flash Forward*, 2007), the Family Tree Gallery in London (*Death in the Peak District*, 2006), and Pacific Switchboard in Portland, Oregon (*Small Business of Bermondsey*, 2004), to name a few.
www.maxinebeuret.com
PHOTO © STEVE BAKER

Chris Buck took up photography when he found pushing a button easier than doing pencil drawings. The results were encouraging. He moved to New York in 1990 and soon found himself with an agent, Julian Richards, with whom he shared an affection for deservedly obscure folk bands. Chris's clients include Microsoft, Citibank, Moviefone, *GQ, Entertainment Weekly, Esquire*, and *New York Magazine*. He is married to Michelle Golden, a senior editor at Zagat, who introduces him to eateries outside of his local red sauce joint. He keeps a second home in Los Angeles, where he spends part of his work time. Chris has been described as "clever" and "damaged," but Werner Herzog put it best when he said, "I will not be posing with your rooster prop."
www.chrisbuck.com
PHOTO © MICHELLE GOLDEN

Julien Capmeil is a contributing photographer to *Condé Nast Traveler* based in New York. He has traveled everywhere from Miami, Florida, to Bangalore, India, in search of the perfect shot.
www.barbaralaurie.com

Pierre Crocquet was born in Cape Town and grew up in Klerksdorp, South Africa, a conservative farming and mining town to the west of Johannesburg. After school, he studied at the University of Cape Town and graduated with a degree in finance. He worked for a time in various London merchant banks but, dissatisfied with his career, abandoned banking to study photography at the London College of Printing, after which he returned to South Africa. His earlier work focused on life in Africa, highlighting the more humorous, romantic, and quirky aspects of living on the continent. His second book, *On Africa Time*, showcases images from eight African countries—Nigeria, Tanzania, Malawi, Mozambique, South Africa, Namibia, Zambia, and Angola.
www.pierrecrocquet.com

Jim Erickson has been a commercial photographer for over twenty years, creating timeless imagery for numerous clients including AT&T, American Express, Bank of America, and L. L. Bean. A native of Eau Claire, Wisconsin, Jim received formal training in photography at the Rochester Institute of Technology. In 1991 he relocated to San Francisco, where he could pursue his career in a larger market. Later he moved to Petaluma, located in Sonoma County, where he and his business reside today.
www.jimerickson.com
PHOTO © TYLER JACOBSEN

Thayer Allyson Gowdy grew up in Connecticut, and understands preppy. Living in California, she understands sunshine. She has one husband, two cats, one snowboard, twenty-three potted plants, and seven pairs of flip-flops. Her suitcase rarely gets unpacked between assignments. She loves flying, chocolate, and mangoes. Her family lives on sixty-five acres in Vermont, and she enjoys snowshoeing on holiday. Her parents are both chefs and her brothers like to work on their trucks. She loves to take pictures. Her clients include *Real Simple, Self*, and *Travel + Leisure* magazines. She shoots everywhere, all the time, but Thayer calls San Francisco home. The light is better there than in Los Angeles, and the grass is greener.
www.thayerphoto.com
PHOTO © AMANDA MARSALIS

Dirk Kikstra graduated from Brooks Institute of Photography in Santa Barbara, CA, in 1997, and shortly after moved to New York City to pursue a career in photography. There he assisted numerous commercial and fashion photographers, including Patrick Demarchelier. In 1999, Kikstra received the offer of a lifetime, to work full-time for the legendary Richard Avedon. He worked with Avedon for more than four years, and the skills he learned continue to help him in his own photography. Kikstra moved to Amsterdam in 2005. His current client list includes the Dutch editions of *Cosmopolitan, Elle, Glamour*, and *Marie Claire*.
www.dirkkikstra.com
PHOTO © CHLOE KIKSTRA

Seth Kushner, a Brooklyn native and self-professed pop culture addict, is often unable to complete sentences without making some reference to *The Simpsons*. Since graduating from New York's School of Visual Arts in 1995, Seth has been assigned by magazines to shoot an eclectic variety of subjects, from businessmen and politicians, to hip-hop artists and DJs. His clients include *The New York Times Magazine, YRB, ESPN the Magazine*, and *Men's Health*.
www.sethkushner.com
PHOTO © TERRA KUSHNER

Vincent Laforet is a Pulitzer Prize–winning commercial and editorial photographer who is regularly commissioned to work on a variety of fine art, advertising, corporate, and editorial projects. His work has been published in major publications worldwide, including *National Geographic*, *TIME*, *Newsweek*, and *Sports Illustrated*. In 2006, Laforet became the first national contract photographer at *The New York Times*. His photographs have been exhibited at the International Center of Photography in New York City and Visa Pour L'Image in Perpignan.
www.vincentlaforet.com

David McLain, who is based in Portland, Maine, has honed his craft shooting feature-length assignments for magazines like *National Geographic*, *National Geographic Adventure*, *National Geographic Traveler*, *Smithsonian*, and *Outside*. Over the past several years, he has shot assignments in New Zealand, Australia, Japan, China, Central and South America, Greenland, and British Columbia. His commercial clients include US Airways, The Nature Conservancy, Eastern Mountain Sports, and the American Skiing Company.
www.davidmclain.com
PHOTO © ANNE MCLAIN

Paul Nicklen is a photographer who grew up in Baffin Island in the territory of Nunavut, Canada, where his family was one of the few non-Inuit families in a small settlement of 140 Inuit. The Inuit taught Nicklen how to survive in the Arctic, read the weather, and most of all, have patience—skills he has put to good use while working as a wildlife biologist for four years in the Northwest Territories, and continues to use as a nature photographer while shooting various assignments for *National Geographic*. Nicklen lives in the country outside of Whitehorse, Yukon, with his wife, Lyn Hartley, and their dog, Bo.
www.paulnicklen.com
PHOTO © CHRIS COLBOURNE

Sara Remington was raised in upstate New York and moved to California after years of being trapped in piles of snow. She is currently working on a cookbook about Rancho Gordo heirloom beans, a book about seasonal drinks at Cyrus Restaurant in Healdsburg, as well as a cookbook about the Big Sur Bakery. She also has an ongoing personal project titled "Swordfish," for which she is photographing hundreds of nostalgic objects from her grandparents' old house in upstate New York. When she's not shooting photos, you can find Sara climbing rocks all over California, driving up and down the coast on Highway 1, and enjoying anchovies and a really stinky cheese.
www.sararemington.com
PHOTO © SARA REMINGTON

F. Scott Schafer is a New York–based photographer who has been shooting celebrities, musicians, and ad campaigns for the last fourteen years. Scott has photographed Johnny Depp, Liv Tyler, Snoop Dogg, Toby McGuire, and Heidi Klum, to name but a few. His advertising clients include NBC Universal, Nike, and MTV, and his photographs have appeared in magazines such as *Vanity Fair*, *Rolling Stone*, and *Blender*.
www.fscottschafer.com
PHOTO © JAMEL TOPPIN

Alys Tomlinson studied at the University of Leeds, UK, and Central Saint Martins College of Art & Design in London. She is based in London and combines commissioned work for editorial, design, and advertising clients with personal work, which she publishes and exhibits. Her commercial clients include *House and Garden*, *Time Out London*, Penguin Books, and John Brown Publishing.
www.alystomlinson.co.uk

Ami Vitale is an independent journalist based in New Delhi, India. Her photographs and stories from events in Europe, the Middle East, and Africa have appeared in *TIME*, *Newsweek*, *U.S. News and World Report*, *BusinessWeek*, *The Guardian*, *The Telegraph Sunday Magazine*, *The New York Times*, *Los Angeles Times*, *USA Today*, and MSNBC, among others. She has extensive experience with transmitting photos and reports from remote locations.
www.amivitale.com
PHOTO © PABLO CORRAL

Matthew Wakem is a New York–based photographer who has spent the past fifteen years traveling around North Africa, Asia, Jamaica, Latin America, and his native New Zealand. His clients include *Condé Nast Traveler*, *Luxury Spa Finder*, The Four Seasons, Ford, *Life*, and *Men's Journal*. When not taking pictures, Wakem has a successful career as a world beat DJ and recently released his first album as a music producer, *The Bambu Brothers*.
www.matthewwakem.com
PHOTO © DIRK KIKSTRA

Ben Watts was born in London and began his picture-taking career in Australia, first working as a photographer's assistant, then shooting on his own for clients, including Australian *Elle* and *Vogue*, among others. Fascinated by American hip-hop culture, he came to New York in 1990 and started documenting urban youth. He has since shot advertising campaigns for Nike, Polo Ralph Lauren, Roxy Quicksilver, Sony Music, and Apple, to name a few. His work has appeared in numerous publications including *Rolling Stone*, *Vibe*, *Esquire*, and *Tokion*.
www.benwatts.com
PHOTO © CHARLEY GALLAY/GETTY IMAGES

Art Wolfe has worked on every continent and in hundreds of locations during his thirty-year career. His stunning images interpret and record the world's fast-disappearing wildlife, land-scapes, and native cultures and are a lasting inspiration to those who seek to preserve them all. In 2000, Wolfe founded Wildlands Press (WP) in Seattle to publish numerous books, including *The Living Wild*, which has sold more than 50,000 copies worldwide, and *Edge of the Earth, Corner of the Sky*, which won the Independent Publisher (IPPY), Benjamin Franklin, and National Outdoor book awards. Wolfe has also ventured into television produc-tion with *On Location with Art Wolfe*, *Techniques of the Masters*, and PBS's *Travels to the Edge with Art Wolfe*.
www.artwolfe.com
www.travelstotheedge.com
PHOTO © JOHN GREENGO / EDGE OF THE EARTH

Photo Speak

A Cheat Sheet to Some Common Photography Terms

Adapter ring: A circular mount, available in several sizes, that enables an accessory, such as a filter, to be used with a lens of a different diameter.

Ambient light: The natural light illuminating a scene.

Aperture: A circular hole in the front of the camera lens that controls the amount of light allowed to pass through to the film or digital sensor.

Aperture Priority mode (A or Av): A setting on most cameras, both film and digital, that allows the photographer to set the aperture while the camera automatically sets the shutter speed.

Aperture ring: A ring located on the outside of the lens, usually behind the focusing ring, that allows the photographer to control the size of the aperture.

ASA: A system of rating photographic materials. Originally devised by the American Standards Association, this rating system has now been replaced by ISO (see definition on p.142 below). Both acronyms are typically followed by a number and refer to film speed.

Autofocus (AF): A built-in device found in most cameras, both film and digital, that focuses the image automatically. An AF sensor is found in most cameras, both digital and film.

Available light: The light normally occurring in a scene, whether natural or artificial.

Blowup: An enlargement of a print relative to the size of the original negative or digital file. The higher the megapixel number of a camera, or the slower the film speed, the more detail it can capture, and the larger you can blow up your image without it appearing blurry.

Blur: Unsharp image areas typically caused by subject or camera movement, or by selective or inaccurate focusing.

Bokeh: Effect achieved when highlights that are out of focus appear as disks of light, lending a background glow to the shot. From the Japanese word *bokeaji*, meaning blur.

Bounce (as in, to bounce light): To direct light toward or away from the subject using a reflective surface.

Bulb (B): A setting on the shutter dial indicating that the shutter will stay open for as long as the release is pressed.

Burning: A common practice in traditional film darkrooms where the negative is printed from back to front, so that increasing the light or "burning" an area of a print makes it appear darker in the final image. This look is simulated in Photoshop using the "Dodge and Burn" tool. (See also Dodging, opposite page.)

Cable release: A camera accessory that enables the photographer to take a picture without touching the camera, using a cable attached to the shutter release button of traditional film cameras or slides of digital cameras allowing the photographer to shoot from a distance.

Camera angle: The position or orientation from which the camera captures a subject or scene.

Camera shake: A common problem in image capture that occurs when the camera is unstable, the ISO is too low for the amount of light, or the shutter is open for an extended period of time (slow shutter speed), causing the image to appear blurry or smeared.

Capture: To record a photographic subject, most often in a digital format. To acquire text, images, audio, and video in their original format in a computer.

Catchlight: The reflection of a light source in a subject's eyes.

CMYK: Cyan-magenta-yellow-black. The four-color system standard widely used for commercial colored printing in which all colors are created from a mixture of these hues.

Collage: A collection of diverse materials—photographs, paper clippings, et al.—assembled to create a unified artistic piece.

Color balance: The standard for creating a print or digital file that matches the color of the original scene.

Color contrast: The perceived difference in a color when surrounded by another color.

Compact camera: A small, portable camera with a built-in lens.

Continuous Shooting mode: Allows you to press down on your shutter to take a rapid succession of shots. In traditional cameras, an autowinder can be used to advance the film automatically.

Crop: In photographic printing or image-editing software, to purposefully omit or cut off certain parts of an image in order to improve its composition.

Darkroom: A lightproof room for the traditional processing and printing of film negatives.

Depth of field: The area behind and in front of the main subject in a photograph that also appears sharp, or in focus.

Diffuse (as in, to diffuse light): To soften or scatter light in order to eliminate harsh contrasts.

Digital zoom: A magnification feature that uses one of two methods: crops the edges of an image so that the final image appears more close up; or stretches an image larger than its original size, usually resulting in a final image that appears much blurrier than the nonzoomed photo. (See page 13 for more on digital zoom).

Documentary photography: Capturing images in order to provide a record of social or political situations, with the aim of conveying information or telling a story.

Dodging: A common practice in traditional film darkrooms in which light is blocked or prevented from reaching the photographic paper, causing that area of the final print image to appear lighter. This look is simulated in editing software like Photoshop, using the "Dodge and Burn" tool. (See also Burning, previous page.)

Double exposure: Two images appearing in the same frame (or on the same negative) so that they are superimposed.

Environmental portrait: A photograph of a person in which the surroundings play an important role in revealing something about the subject's character and life.

Exposure: The process of light hitting the surface of some light-sensitive material, such as film or photographic paper or a digital image sensor. Determined by shutter speed, lens aperture, and film speed. Also, the individual shots taken on a roll of film.

Exposure value (EV): A scale of values (also known as light value) used to indicate the amount of light hitting the surface of a photosensitive material; based on a combination of shutter speed and aperture values. For example, EV 0 is the combination of a one-second exposure at $f/1$. This value scale is often used on older cameras and light meters.

Fill light: A light or source of illumination used to bring out shadowy areas. Fill-in flash is one example.

Film: A photographic material that consists of a thin, transparent plastic base coated with a light-sensitive emulsion.

Film speed: The sensitivity of film or a digital sensor (in digital cameras) to light. Film speed is measured by ASA or ISO.

Filter: Colored glass, gelatin (gel), or plastic discs that modify the light passing through them to give the resulting image a tinted hue. Filters can be placed directly on a lens, or the look can be simulated during post-processing using the "Filter" tool of most image-editing software programs.

Flash: An artificial light source that gives brief but very bright illumination. Can be built into the camera or be portable, attaching to camera's hot shoe.

Focal length: The distance, in millimeters, from the optical center of the lens to the image sensor when the lens is focused on infinity. This distance determines the lens' angle of view, or how much your camera can see. For example, a 21–35mm lens is a wide-angle lens, and is ideal for landscapes. An 85mm lens is good for portraits. A camera system whose lens cannot be interchanged for a lens of different focal length is said to have a fixed focal length lens.

Focal point: The exact point at which the camera is focused for maximum sharpness.

Focus: The position at which rays of light converge to form a sharp image.

Frame: A single exposure on a roll of film. In the camera, the viewfinder's image boundary.

Frames per second (fps): The measurement used to describe how many frames a motor drive can handle automatically, or how many times the shutter can open and close within a given second to capture images. Motion pictures are made using high-number fps.

f-stop: A number that represents the aperture (opening) of a lens. A large opening is a small f-stop number, and a small opening is a large f-stop number. (See page 16 for more on f-stops.)

Grain: Clumps of silver halide in film and paper that constitute the image. These grains are produced both in the exposure process (film grain) and in the development process (paper grain). An image with little grain typically refers to an image with sharp, fine details. A grainy image appears coarser, or speckled, and the details are less evident.

Highlight: The brightest areas of the subject.

Histogram: A graphic representation of how brightness and darkness pixels are distributed in an image that can be viewed on the LCD screen or electronic viewfinder of most digital cameras. It indicates whether or not an image is properly exposed. Skewed heavily to the left, it indicates a dark image, while a histogram skewed heavily to the right indicates a light image.

Hot shoe: The fitting on the top of many cameras, with an electrical contact, onto which a photographer can attach a portable flash.

Hot spot: An often undesirable concentration of brightness in a particular area of an image. An area of overexposure.

Image-editing software: Computer programs such as Adobe Photoshop, Picasa, and Gimp that allow you to enhance captured images by adjusting brightness, contrast, color saturation, and hue. Also can be used to create imaginary images.

Image resolution: The amount of data stored in an image file, measured in ppi (pixels per inch) or dpi (dots per inch). A larger ppi or dpi number indicates a higher image quality.

Image sensor: The device in digital cameras and camcorders used to detect an image.

IS (image stabilization): A built-in technical feature found in higher-end digital cameras and lenses that reduces camera shake, allowing you to handhold the camera in situations that would normally require a tripod to produce a sharp image.

ISO: A system devised by the International Standards Organization, widely used in place of ASA to rate film speeds.

JPEG: A format for compressed graphics files. Named after the Joint Photographic Experts Group, JPEG files are the most common image format used for photography on the Web; it is also the default format used by almost every digital camera ever made.

Key light: The main subject-illuminating light source, particularly in a studio situation.

Lamp: A general term used to describe the various kinds of artificial light sources used in photography.

Landscape: Horizontal orientation of a photograph while shooting or in print. Also, subject of a picture taken outdoors, of a natural scene, often with a wide-angle lens.

Large-format camera: Any camera having a picture format of 4 × 5 inches or larger.

LCD: The liquid crystal display screen found on many digital cameras that allows the previewing or reviewing of images.

Lens: An optical element made of glass or plastic and capable of bending light. A lens may be constructed of single or multiple elements. It can be built into the camera or interchangeable, with different focal lengths.

Lens hood: A round rubber or plastic shade that attaches to the front end of a lens, to shield it from unwanted light.

Lightbox: A box containing fluorescent tubes balanced for white light and covered with translucent glass or plastic; used for viewing prints, film negatives, transparencies, or slides.

Light meter: Also referred to as an exposure meter, an instrument for measuring the amount of light falling on, or being reflected by, a subject. Most cameras on the market have a built-in light meter, but handheld light meters are available.

Macro lens: A lens specially designed to allow for extreme close-ups, magnifying the subject, and producing an image that is much larger than the original subject's size.

Manual mode: A camera setting that allows the photographer to custom-adjust aperture and shutter speed.

Mosaic: A singular image that is actually made up of numerous smaller images.

Negative: The image produced on a photographic emulsion by the product of exposure and development, in which tones are reversed so that highlights appear dark and shadows appear light.

Noise: In digital imagery and digital photography, used to describe the occurrence of color dots or specks where there should be none.

Overexposure: A term used to indicate that too much light has affected your photograph, resulting in a whitish, washed-out image.

Painting with light: A photographic technique in which images are captured at night or in a darkroom by moving a light source, such as a flashlight, to illuminate an entire scene or parts of a subject.

Panning: A photographic technique used to capture moving subjects. While the shutter is open, the camera is swung in the same direction in which the subject is moving. This creates a blurred background but a sharp subject.

Pixels: Picture elements, or minute squares of light that make up a digital image. One megapixel equals one million pixels. The higher the megapixel number of a camera, the more detail it can capture; digital models typically range from 2 to 15 megapixels.

Point-and-shoot: A film or digital camera in which the focus and exposure are completely automatic.

Polaroid: A camera (trademark) that produces developed pictures instantly. The term also refers to the actual instant pictures.

Portrait: Vertical orientation of a photograph as seen through the viewfinder or in print. Also, genre of photography where person is the main subject; common types include the head-and-shoulder shot, environmental portrait, and self-portrait.

RAW: Large-file format digital image, favored by professional photographers. An uncompressed, unprocessed picture that allows the photographer to do all the processing in a computer after downloading the images.

Red eye: An unwanted photographic effect that results in the appearance of red pupils in a subject's eyes. Red eye typically occurs when using a flash very close to the camera lens in low light, simultaneous with the shutter opening, as with most compact cameras.

Reflector: Any device (usually a white or gray card) used to redirect light onto a subject in order to soften it and to eliminate harsh shadows.

Retouching: An after-capture treatment carried out on a negative or digital image in order to remove blemishes, improve color, and generally enhance the original shot.

Ring flash: A ring-shaped electronic flash unit attached to the front of a lens, used to give even frontal lighting in close-up situations.

Saturation: The purity or intensity of color in an image.

Selective focus: A method of adjusting the lens aperture to give a depth of field that will confine image sharpness to a particular area of the image.

Self-timer: A mechanism for delaying the opening of the shutter for a given number of seconds after the release has been operated.

Sensitivity: The degree to which a film or digital sensor is affected by exposure to light.

Shutter: A mechanical camera component that opens and closes at adjustable speeds to control the time that light is allowed to act on the film or digital sensor.

Shutter lag: The time that elapses between pressing the shutter release button and when the camera takes the picture. On many SLRs, about 0.1 seconds; on compact cameras, significantly longer.

Shutter Priority mode (TV or S): A camera setting in which the photographer selects the shutter speed, and the camera automatically sets an appropriate aperture size.

Shutter speed: The measurement of the action of the shutter that controls the duration of an exposure. The faster the speed, the shorter the exposure. Shutter speed settings are in seconds (1 sec., 1/15 sec., 1/500 sec., etc.)

Single-lens reflex (SLR): A term associated with 35mm, medium-format film, or digital cameras; SLR cameras use a mirror between the lens and the film, or image sensor, to provide a focus screen. Thus, the image you see in the viewfinder (or LCD) will be the same as what appears on film or digitally.

Slow sync: A flash technique in which the flash is used in conjunction with a slow shutter speed to capture ambient light.

Softbox: A standalone light, enclosed in translucent material, used to diffuse and soften light.

Spotlight: An artificial light source used to produce a strong beam of light of controllable width.

Still life: The depiction of inanimate subject matter, most typically a small grouping of commonplace objects, arranged to make full use of form, shape, and lighting.

Stock photo: Online photo libraries of images shot mostly by professional photographers from all over the world. Magazines, newspapers, advertising agencies can access these libraries and purchase the use of an image. Major examples are Getty Images and Corbis, but there are many microstock agencies as well.

Stopping down: Changing the lens aperture to a smaller opening (larger f-stop number) such as f/8 or f/12, so that more of the subject is in focus owing to greater depth of field.

Strobe: A flash that can fire repeatedly at regular, controlled intervals.

T (Time): A shutter speed setting used for timed exposures of longer duration than the numbered settings. The shutter opens when the release is pressed and closes when it is pressed again. Now largely replaced by the B (bulb) setting.

Teleconverter: An optical system mounted between a camera body and the lens, serving to increase the effective focal length of the lens.

Telephoto lens: A fixed-length photographic lens or lens system used to produce a larger, more close-up image of a faraway object.

TIFF: Tagged image file format. Like a JPEG, a TIFF is a form of compressed image and is widely used by desktop publishing companies.

Tripod: A three-legged camera support of adjustable height.

TTL (through the lens) metering: A system in which a light meter within the camera body measures exposure from the image-forming light that has passed through the lens.

Underexposure: A condition in which too little light reaches the film or digital sensor, producing a dark or muddy-looking image.

Viewfinder: A device on a camera that previews, either optically or electronically, what will appear in the field of vision of the lens.

Vignetting: A printing or digital image manipulation technique in which the edges of the picture are gradually faded out to black or white. Also refers to a falloff in illumination at the edge of an image, such as may be caused by a lens hood or similar attachment partially blocking the field of view of the lens.

White balance: The process of removing unrealistic color casts so that objects that appear white in person are rendered white in your photograph.

Wide-angle lens: A lens whose focal length is substantially shorter than that of a normal lens in relation to the image or negative size produced by the camera.

Wide-area autofocus (AF): Indicates that the autofocus detection area is wider than normal, making it easier to photograph moving subjects.

Zoom lens: An optical zoom is a true zoom lens whose focal length extends and retracts so that an image is magnified while the image resolution stays the same. A digital zoom simulates optical zooming by targeting the center of the picture, cropping the surrounding area, and enlarging the subject to appear closer in the frame.

Zoom panning: A feature on some SLRs that allows you to take a photograph (e.g., at 1/40 sec.) while zooming in on the subject. The photo will show blurred movement toward the center of the image, which can give it a dramatic appearance.

Index